THINKING out *LOUD*

Collected scripts from Radio 4's 'Thought For The Day'

John L. Bell

WILD GOOSE PUBLICATIONS

www.ionabooks.com

THINKING out *LOUD*

In tribute to
Tam Bell and Murn Neil,
my grandparents,
who endured much
but enabled more.

Contents

Introduction

The scripts

Introduction

The two-minutes-forty-seconds' segment in BBC Radio 4's *Today* programme entitled 'Thought for the Day' is essentially an exercise in thinking out loud.

It takes place over halfway through a three-hour flagship news and current affairs programme of national importance whose presenters are among the most intelligent, well-informed, skilful and deft of British broadcasters.

It is not the place for biblical exposition or evangelical polemic. Contributors are expected to comment on a current news story from their own faith perspective to a listening audience whose primary concerns at 7.50 in the morning will probably have little to do with religion. The topic will have been agreed the day before, but may be subject to amendment until the last minute.

Sometime in 2001, Christine Morgan, a producer in the Religion Department of BBC Manchester, asked if I would consider being a contributor. I deferred the invitation, expecting thereby to be forgotten. But a year later she came back with the same request, and with some apprehension I agreed.

Although I have occasionally broadcast on radio and television for almost 30 years, I have never regarded it as an ambition or even a fascination. Communicating in person is more my passion, whether through seminars or preaching. But I have always regarded radio as a preferable medium to television in that it affords the listener a reciprocal kind of engagement. When only the ears are engaged, reflection and disagreement are much easier than when a screen offering sound and vision demands one's fuller attention. The 'Thoughts for the Day' printed here are, with little amendment, the words which were first read on the airwaves. Four exceptions are scripts which were prepared but were not broadcast, as sometimes happens if a significant item of news breaking on the previous evening requires a new script or another contributor. The disparity in frequency is all to do with my being away from home up to seven months a year, thus making a commitment to three successive weekly contributions not the easiest of requests to fulfil.

There is also an appendix: the transcript of a lecture I gave in Bristol in the autumn of 2006 in which I attempted to identify some of the roots of my concern that the Christian faith should engage its adherents with the world rather than encourage them to deny its importance.

This book would not have appeared had individuals not written for copies of scripts and publishers suggested a collection in one volume. I am indebted to these parties for their encouragement. But I am more indebted to the staff of the BBC Religion Department, particularly Christine Morgan, David Coombes, Amanda Hancox and Norman Winter, whose professionalism and skill as editors is as encouraging as it is enviable. Thanks are also generously due to Rosemary Grundy who coordinates contributions in Manchester, to Gail Ullrich, our administrator in Glasgow, who checked every text and sent it down the wire, and to Sandra Kramer, the publishing manager of Wild Goose Publications, who edited the manuscripts.

John L. Bell

The scripts

The need to speak in tongues

... a consequence of global citizenry

I should not have been surprised at 5.15 yesterday morning to hear a voice saying, 'Excuse me sir, do you have a ticket?' But I was.

I was on a train travelling between Uppsala and Stockholm, and the motherly conductor was Swedish. But she addressed me in English because she saw the cover of the magazine I was reading.

I wondered for a moment whether, had I been travelling from London to Manchester with a *Paris Match* on the table, the conductor would have said, 'Pardonnez-moi, Monsieur, mais avez-vous un billet?'

My cynicism got its come-uppance later in the day on a flight from Amsterdam to Glasgow. It was a distinctly Scottish voice that said,
'Dames en Herren, heertilijk welkom aan bord.'
... and then told us in Dutch how to buckle our seat-belts.

Then, as we were flying across the North Sea, I read in my newspaper that while the Prime Minister was meeting Mr Chirac in France the other day, the education ministers of both countries signed an agreement to improve language teaching by exchanges, twinning of schools and internet links.

What a change from the wisdom of my grandfather who advised that, when speaking to foreigners, it was sufficient to shout at them in order to be understood!

Of course, for native English speakers, the prospect of learning another language often carries more dread than novelty. We presume that everyone else should want to speak like us. And the ease with which Dutch, Belgian and Scandinavian nationals lapse into English encourages us to believe that there is really no need for us to return the compliment.

And so we miss out.

For with language comes cultural assumptions and with these assumptions comes a particular world-view ... and how impoverished we are if we believe that ours is the only way of looking at life.

Yet how much richer we are if we can see the truth from more than one perspective. Then we might not call the French or Germans or Arabs stupid if they don't see things the way we do.

I was persuaded of this both through working in another European nation for two years, and through once hearing the Japanese theologian Kosuke Koyama. He spoke of what it felt like to move from perceiving God through oriental eyes, to teaching and worshipping in the USA. He argued that the colossal language and culture change was much more of a blessing than a curse. For in the transition he discovered that the 'mother-tongue God was too small'.

If God is God and truth is true, surely there is nothing but gain when another language opens other windows into reality.

So, well done this new *entente cordiale* ... in token of which I will not have porridge today for breakfast, but croissants and café noir.

6 Feb 03

Consternation in the comfort zone

… or the consequences of living in a democracy

I feel for the 6,000 residents of Lee-on-the-Solent in Hampshire whose Anglo-Saxon tranquillity is under threat. It seems that the former naval barracks on their doorstep is to be used as an accommodation centre for asylum-seekers. Fears of the village becoming a terrorist resort and of house prices falling have sent blood pressure soaring.

One native, however, is reported as suggesting a novel alternative location for the asylum-seekers, namely the Outer Hebrides … until they have been 'processed'.

I'm sure this will be sweet music to Gaelic ears in Lewis and Harris where house prices are not so high. Maybe a swap could be done. Maybe the Royal Air Force which sends its low-flying jets along valleys like the Strath of Kildonan and over the Western Isles could reroute its planes to screech above the leafy glades of Hampshire instead.

Or maybe the asylum-seekers' centre could be located in Faslane, in return for which Britain's pristine and highly dangerous nuclear base could be located in the much more accessible waters of the Solent.

Or maybe the asylum-seekers could go to Peterhead, and the sex-offenders' unit at the local prison could move to where the inmates would get a lovely view of the Isle of Wight rather than the dreich waters of the North Sea.

What is this – a racist rant by a deranged nationalist? No. I'm sure that the unnamed plaintive from Lee-on-the-Solent is not a deranged nationalist. Nor am I. But we may represent different understandings of what both faith and democracy are about.

As regards democracy, any nation has to deal with unavoidable and unpopular issues such as the care of those who are insane, criminal or seeking asylum. And the same democracy, if it possesses nuclear weapons and nuclear power plants, has to decide where they will be located. It seems to me quite unfair that people who want the benefits of a democracy should want to exempt themselves from taking their share of the negatives just because they have money.

And as regards faith, I don't see any of the world religions and certainly not Christianity promoting earthly refuges to avoid the rawness of life. Faith in God is not about finding how to exempt ourselves from what is awkward but about enabling us to deal with the contradictions and rough edges of existence.

But then, I suppose I would have to say that, not because I'm paid to but because Christ himself was an asylum-seeker and spoke of affection for God being demonstrated in how we receive or reject the stranger among us.

13th Feb 03

Supping with the so-called devil

… or choosing between dialogue and demonisation

So the French have done it again … slapped Britain's diplomatic face by allowing Robert Mugabe into Europe to talk about the future of Africa. This is the man who – like Saddam Hussein – has a human rights record which would make Genghis Khan blush. And the French want to talk to him!

'Thank God we're British!' do I hear someone say? 'We wouldn't dialogue with dictators or terrorists.'

'Why not?' I want to ask. What is it that would make us refuse to talk to such adversaries? Is it the fear that we might be seen to condone their actions? In which case Tory MPs shouldn't drink in the same parliamentary bar as their Labour counterparts.

Is it that the spectre of appeasement might raise its head … as if compromise is universally wrong and accusation unilaterally right? Or is it that in dialogue we might hear what we don't want to listen to?

Is it that Mugabe might ask,
   'Why did Harold Wilson come to talk to Ian Smith thirty years ago, but no one comes to negotiate with me?'

Is it that Mugabe might say,
   'Your civil war in Northern Ireland began to change direction when you took the so called "terrorists" seriously. Why do you not use that tactic elsewhere?'

Is it that Saddam might ask,
'Why did the great Rumsfeld want to consolidate and arm me over twenty years ago but wants to depose and disarm me now?'

Or might Saddam enquire,
'Why have four million Iraqi exiles suddenly become a pretext for war? Is it because your other arguments are failing?'

I have no affection for Mugabe or Saddam or any other dictator. I deplore their brutality. But I am also aware that demonisation is a convenient substitute for dialogue, especially if you are convinced of your own self-righteousness.

And I suppose I sit uneasily under the command 'Love your enemies'. I've always regarded that as an ethic for personal relations, not a maxim for international diplomacy.

But since it is the *West* which has portrayed both Mugabe and Saddam as personal tyrants, maybe the personal ethic comes back into play.

To love the neighbour doesn't require our leaders to French-kiss their Iraqi or Zimbabwean counterparts. But it does require that they be treated as persons and not things. You cannot dialogue with an object and change it or be changed; but the engagement of minds and the meeting of people has infinite potential.

20 Feb 03

cultural heritage

Lust of possession

... the need to preserve a wealth for all nations

'If I cannot always find the words, you will know that my heart is still speaking.'

... this was how Donny George began to address an international gathering of experts on ancient art in London on Tuesday. He is the curator of the Baghdad Museum and was talking about the irreparable damage done by looters.

'If I cannot always find the words, you will know that my heart is still speaking.'

He sounded full of grief, but what was he grieving for? Was it simply the loss of irreplaceable treasures like the 5000-year-old Wark Vase? Was it the undoing of a lifetime's work in curating?

Or was he also grieved by what the English poet Laurence Houseman called 'the lust of possession'?

On the surface of it, there is a major contrast between the Ministry of Oil being defended in Baghdad, while fifty yards from a tank unit a museum containing world treasures was being looted. But there's also a similarity in these two activities. Both have to do with Houseman's 'lust of possession', and specifically with the desire of one party to take to itself what should be available to all.

In the case of the professional looters, they took the gems of a nation's cultural heritage to place in private hands. In the case of the Oil Ministry, it's hard *not* to think that it was staunchly defended because the USA relies on the Middle East for almost a third of its petroleum. And, doubtless, America will want to maintain its privileged level of consumption, whereby the average US family uses as much fossil fuel in 48 hours as the average Tanzanian family does in a year.

There's a common thread running through all the world religions which recognises that the gifts of the past should be for the welfare of the future, and that the finite commodities of the earth are for the benefit of all.

Jesus articulated this in stories about rich men whose ability to hoard or consume was in stark contrast to the poverty of those at their gates who could barely survive. That which nourishes life is intended, by God, for all.

And in our present context, that should speak as directly to the appropriation of natural resources as to the looting of cultural heritage. Otherwise in the museums of the future, it will not be Babylonian treasures our grandchildren look at, but that odd obsolete black liquid which the privileged and powerful West guzzled up through its obsession with, and dependence on, private transport.

1st May 03

The meaning of life

... as reflected in a popular sentence

Good morning ... Or should I say 'cheers'?

For according to the Home Secretary speaking yesterday on the *Today* programme, that's what we should be doing – cheering.

And the cause of the celebration? – the new sentencing principles being proposed by Mr Blunkett whereby, for child murderers 'life' means life, and for those found guilty of other horrendous crimes, sentences of thirty years or more may be mandatory.

So, cheers! ... And there will be cheering, or at least murmurs of approval, that at last we have a Home Secretary who is tough on criminals.

I would also cheer if I believed that longer sentences – or even the death penalty – were as effective in deterring crime as they are in making the hang-them-and-flog-them brigade feel smug. But there's little evidence. Nor is there much evidence that the prison system, already groaning with over 73,000 inmates, enables offenders to reform and become law-abiding members of society. While crime rates have fallen, reoffending rates have not.

Indeed, it's quite ironic that the USA and Britain which have recently joined forces as global policemen are the very nations which, among the democracies of the world, have the highest proportions of their population behind bars.

Like the Home Secretary, I believe that 'life' should mean life, but I think of that not as a slogan for a voter-friendly penal policy. I regard it as a central issue of Christian faith.

Among the few claims he made for himself, Jesus said,
'I have come that you might have life
and have it abundantly.'

He was not speaking as a magistrate, he was speaking as a lover of the world and its people. He was speaking as one who was concerned that men and women should not live diminished lives in which their talents never flourish but fulfilled lives in which their worth is attested, and their potential maximised. And that, in my book, applies to criminals as much as it applies to cabinet ministers.

I don't have a wide range of acquaintances in the prison population, but I have one friend who served ten years for child murder and another who served ten years for armed robbery. One has reoffended and is back inside, the other lives in a state of permanent paranoia.

I don't deny that society had a right to punish them. And I don't believe that the Christian faith or any other faith which extols justice would want criminals to be excused from paying the penalty for their actions.

But I do believe that any civilised society, as well as having a right to punish offenders, has an obligation to develop in them the humanity and potential for good which has yet to flower ... if life means life.

8 May 03

Sentiment for what is seen

... and the dispossession of what goes unnoticed

It's amazing how we're wired up.

We hear a politician expounding his party philosophy and we remain unimpressed. But if we see him kiss a baby or shed a tear, we think he's a man to be trusted, so we give him our vote.

Conversely, we hear a vicar espousing the sanctity of married life and feel reassured. But if we see his wife with a black eye, our suspicion of him is immediately aroused.

So, for Iraqi citizens, the rhetoric which has bombarded them via the airwaves and leaflets from the sky about the menace of Saddam may have meant nothing to a people wary of Western propaganda. But when mass graves are exhumed, and the corpses of women and children as well as men and boys summarily shot are exposed to public view, the iniquity of the man is beyond question.

To paraphrase a 20th-century Scottish poet,
    It's sight, not sense
    that moves the hearts of all.

And it may be that we too are moved, moved by the sight of weeping women cradling plastic bags of rotten bones, moved to a sense of smug indignation that the war was justified and that we were right all along, moved even to forget that the reasons for the war had to do with the assumed link between Al Qaeda and Saddam, and the presumed possession of weapons of mass destruction – neither of which conjectures has, as yet, been fully vindicated.

Still, that doesn't matter. We just feel moved.

But being moved is not enough.

That is what an enthusiastic celebrity-spotter discovered when he heard Jesus speak and saw what he did. He felt so moved that he said he'd like to be a follower, but there was the issue of his father's funeral to take care of first.

And in words which may well offend us, who have seen pictures of exhumed Iraqi corpses, Jesus said,
Leave the dead to bury their dead.
You have to go and announce the kingdom of God.

Was it that Jesus meant to be insensitive and dismissive? Or was it that he discerned in his would-be follower how the sentiment of the moment is insufficient for repairing a broken world?

They won't be exhuming the corpses of their loved ones in Africa today, where 40 million are on the verge of starvation, according to the UN. They will be watching thousands die whose fate could have been different if the gaze of world compassion and the coffers of the West had not been so powerfully focused on a middle-eastern war for the past three months.

Does Africa have to wait until we see pictures and feel moved before a different coalition of the willing prevents other innocents from dying?

15 May 2003

22

Celebrity incarcerations

... with a plea for the less favoured

I wonder who came out of prison this morning?

Nobody famous, I imagine, or we would have known. Not like yesterday morning when a peer of the realm emerged to be reunited with the media who had missed his accessibility for two years.

That gentleman, whom I shall not name, will now be easing himself back into family, employment, property and public life, all of which should ensure that in his case there is no recidivism.

Recidivism – there's a word not suited to loose dentures. It means re-offending. And it's something which is on the increase, despite the overall decrease in the crime rate. And it happens, ironically, because for some prisoners freedom is a bigger threat than incarceration, especially when – unlike our disgraced nobleman – there is no structure to support them on release.

So it was that Tony (not his real name) phoned me around this time last year and said,
     'John, I'm being let out on licence in two hours.
     Can you meet me off the train?'

He had been in jail for a decade. He was 27. He had been given no training for freedom. He had no social skills, he had no idea what money could buy, how to order a hamburger, how to relate to women, how to plan his time. And the only support network he had was a dysfunctional family who dealt in drugs. So now he's back inside for another two years.

An isolated case? No, I could also talk about Billy and Brian whose testimony is similar, but whose plight is not a *cause célèbre*. There's nothing sexy about prison reform; there are few politicians campaigning for the rehabilitation of offenders.

Maybe that's why Jesus was insistent that nations would be judged according to how they dealt with prisoners. And the Bible knows quite a lot about prisoners. Half the New Testament was written from exile or incarceration and the big names like Joseph and Jeremiah and Paul and even Jesus himself were all at one time behind bars.

Nations are judged according to how the most marginalised are cared for rather than condemned, condemnation being the much easier option. For when any group of people – offenders, asylum-seekers or the mentally ill – is disowned by society, that group is likely to be demonised and we all know what happens when you give a dog a bad name.

In the eyes of the media, celebrity prisoners on parole or release are front-page news. In the eyes of God, the humanity of people in Guantanamo Bay and Wormwood Scrubs and Barlinnie is much more important.

Is that Nelson Mandela shouting, 'Hear! Hear!'?

22 July 03

Clocking on before checking in

... or 1984 comes late to Heathrow

As someone who used to clock on and clock off, I have a certain sympathy with the British Airways staff at Heathrow.

There was something strangely satisfying about putting a time-card into a slot, pulling a lever, hearing a bell ping and seeing in bold print that a fair day's work was being recorded in the hope of a fair day's wage.

Swiping an ID card along a grimy aperture doesn't have the same romantic appeal. And if someone should argue that it cuts down the risk of fraud, the argument might hold for a few months. Those intent on fiddling the system will always find alternative strings for their new bow.

The underlying issue here is something which the airline workers have in common with school teachers, academics, GPs and a host of others who never clock on or clock off but who sense themselves mistrusted.

While league tables and performance targets might be seen by some to ensure if not enhance performance, they can as easily be seen by others as indices of suspicion and unnecessary control.

The issue is trust, the trust of a superior in those who are accountable as a means of affirmation and encouragement. It's something which I claim as a Christian virtue, and it's not because I want all the good things to belong to God. It seems to me that in entrusting Christ to the world, God ceases to be Big

Brother watching us, and becomes Big Brother alongside us, valuing us, depending on us and encouraging mutual respect.

And when the Big Brother whom we call Jesus begins to develop his mission in the world, he doesn't secure his disciples' cooperation by legislation and performance targets, he does it by simple trust.

I used to work in a home for delinquent boys, some of whom had been placed there by court order, few of whom would have called themselves trustworthy. And I was always amazed at a practice the warden had with boys who had been guilty of theft.

He would give them an open envelope with between £50 and £100 pounds in it and ask them to pay it into his bank account. And he would do this almost casually, without hedging his bets by indicating what penalties would ensue should any money go missing.

Money never went missing. For these suspected delinquents, the experience of being trusted radically altered the expectations they had of themselves.

Now it would be naive to claim that this situation ethic is automatically transferable to the world of industrial relations. Of course it would be naive. But it is equally naive to believe that performance targets and a battery of precautionary measures against default will bring out the best in those who feel themselves already under suspicion.

29 July 03

children

The advantages of small talk

... in opposition to a Victorian value

On the third stroke it will be a Scottish accent.

A year ago, at the youth centre on the Island of Iona, there were two questions asked by Glasgow teenagers who had just arrived and eaten dinner. The first question was: 'Will we always have home-cooked food?' That was not an irregular enquiry given that today's teenagers have increasingly become used to carry-out meals and microwave dinners.

The second question was more unusual: 'Will we always sit at tables?'

I discussed this with the teacher who had brought the pupils. She said the enquiry did not surprise her as she reckoned that half the children lived in homes where there was no meal table. They either ate in front of television sets or dined alone in their bedrooms, while watching their computer screen.

I mentioned this last week when I was lecturing at a seminary in the USA. Afterwards one of the students told me about an article he had read in an educational journal. It concerned the declining standard of conversational skills in young people. The article indicated that this was not something governed by economic status or social or cultural background, but was mainly the result of fewer parents listening to their children.

The report went on to reveal that a survey had discovered how the first item which American families purchased when setting up home was invariably a television, and the last was a kitchen table.

So what has that to do with how on the third stroke there will be a Scottish accent?

It's simply that the avuncular voice of the talking clock is to be replaced for a week by the sound of Alicia Roland, a twelve-year-old girl from Paisley. This is not a move to rotate regional accents with the hour hands, but a novel attempt to encourage parents to listen to children.

For me, that is a biblical mandate. The only incident in Christ's childhood which is recorded in the Gospels concerns Jesus, at the age of twelve, giving his parents the slip in order to converse with men five times his age in the Jerusalem Temple. The record is quite specific:

They were amazed at his questions
and at the answers he gave.
– a clear indication that the conversation was two-way.

I don't have children, but I frequently stay with families who do, and know from the way children express an interest in the visitor whether or not they are used to talking to their parents. And if I were to make a subjective judgement, it would be that the happiest households and the funniest households are not those where overworked parents watch the clock as they spend in an hour's quality time with their offspring.

They are the homes where, at any hour of the day, parents engage with the questions their children ask, and through conversation are able, with the Jerusalem Temple cognoscenti, to be amazed at the answers even children give.

15 Oct 03

The bondage of busyness
... a plea for taking and making time

There's a marvellous book by the German author Michael Ende. It's called *Momo*; it was written in 1973 and it's about time thieves.

It observes, through the eyes of an outsider, how people are seduced into overwork. And in the process busyness displaces friendship, schedules displace compassion, and the time for others which makes life rich is stolen.

Not long before Ende's novel was published, we had a series of prime ministers who would take afternoon naps, write books, go to the theatre and delight in being *bon viveurs*; and nobody thought it was wrong.

Now, if the present incumbent in Downing Street were known to be playing bridge of an afternoon or went to a West End cinema every Thursday night as a matter of course, there would be an outcry. We expect public servants, especially those who are our political masters, to be dedicated to duty 24 hours a day. And if their health should suffer, then those who yesterday were demanding a pound of flesh will today say take it easy, so that tomorrow the same degree of busyness might be exacted.

Perhaps we expect this of figures in political life because so many of us have bought into or become victims of a stress-obsessed society, and we wouldn't want those at the top to have more time on their hands than we have on ours.

Or perhaps we fear time in the same way as some people fear silence. Not sure of what to do with it, we retreat into busyness and defend ourselves by saying that we are the victims of a demanding job and a full diary.

And in the process time becomes the enemy, and we speak of it in hostile terms: we talk about time beating us, or about having to kill time.

Maybe, for our own good, we should befriend time rather than demonise it. Maybe, just as in our most prudent moments we budget our money and take stock of the consequences of overspending, so we should budget, discuss, decide on and befriend our time.

And maybe part of that process is blowing the whistle on always saying 'yes' and finding the courage sometimes to say 'no'.

Being known as a busy but obliging person and being regarded as indispensable may massage our ego; but such things may also destroy the very ego they flatter.

And if not saying 'yes' every time seems rather 'un-Christian', then maybe we should look again at Christ. Jesus didn't heal everybody who was ill, he never entered every debate that was on offer. But he did know some facts of life which we may have forgotten … namely that God is not a time-thief.

God is a holiday maker; and time is not a threat, it's a gift.

15 Oct 03

Neon deities

... and the worship of domestic consumption

It's a funny old world when the USA which proclaims its faith on every dollar bill is arguing about what to do with God, while Italy, producer of wines with distinctly religious labels such as Lacrimae Christi (the tears of Christ), is unsure of what to do with crucifixes.

I refer, as listeners to yesterday's programme will recognise, to a debate in Italy about the place of religious symbols in schools. It began when a Muslim father objected to the cross being on display where his child was being educated.

In the piece which we heard yesterday, it was plain that most Muslims *did not* want public places to be stripped of Christian symbols, while some ethnic Italians *did* want the crosses removed. Indeed, one woman said that people should make up their own minds about what religious artefacts confront them.

And I actually would agree with her, were it not for two things. The first is a comment made recently by an Islamic scholar at a conference in Derby. He was asked whether Islam feared the West. He replied, 'Islam does not fear the West because Islam is a faith centred on God. But some Muslims fear the West because the West – in its politics and economics – goes out of the way to deny the importance of religion in public life.'

So, for Muslims, the fact that faith is publicly acknowledged is preferable to its being sidestepped.

But there's another issue, namely that irrespective of Christian, Islamic or Hindu beliefs, Western societies are dominated by deities. Unlike in ancient Rome, however, worship of them is more subtle.

We don't have shrines to Mars, the god of war, but we do pay lip service to a huge armaments industry at whose behest children in Angola and Mozambique still lose limbs through tramping on hidden landmines.

We don't have shrines to Mammon, the god of insatiable consumption, but the logos of multinational junk food giants are foisted in the face of the world's poorest, with the expectation of instant devotion.

We don't have shrines to Bacchus and Aphrodite, the deities associated with excess and gratification, but we do have a whole fashion industry committed to exploiting the variable tastes of children and teenagers who don't have the money to pay the dues which the brand names demand. And so pester their parents.

By all means take down the Cross and the Crescent and the Star of David, but only if you also take down the insignia of the multinational commercial powers and predators.

Or else leave the symbols of religious faith in their place, allowing – in the case of the cross – for the self-importance of earthly gods to be set against the seeming naivety of the Creator of the universe who saves the world through suffering love.

29 Oct 03

celebrity

The affirmation of the unfamous

... in a society obsessed with celebrity

I was saddened to hear, on Sunday, of the death of the actor Alan Bates, especially since one of my best cinema memories was watching him years ago in the film *Women in Love.*

And then yesterday the death of Bob Monkhouse was announced, and another door to memories was opened.

And today there's another show-business obituary – that of Dinsdale Landen.

With no disrespect to the deceased, these announcements have led me to muse on how unbalanced it seems that people who have been in the public eye for years are, at their death, sometimes eulogised in more air minutes or column inches than are devoted to murder hunts or scientific discoveries.

Why is it that celebrity status accrues to some and not others?

I mean, if an artificial limb-maker who had brought increased mobility to thousands were to die, there would be no fuss. If a researcher on the cutting edge of finding a cure for multiple sclerosis were to pass away, there wouldn't be a fraction of the attention that's given to film and television stars.

What is it that encourages us to applaud some and under-value others?

I'm reminded of a conversation I had four years ago with two young international lawyers. I asked them if they were the kind of guys who might in ten years' time expect Christmas bonuses in six figures. They replied in the affirmative.

Then I asked one of them: Who do you think most deserves two hundred grand at Christmas – you or the primary school teacher who identified your abilities, and who encouraged you to believe in yourself? There was no answer.

What is it that makes us value people not in proportion to their worth, but in accordance with their financial or celebrity profile?

It's not an issue to which the Bible gives any answer. Because that kind of selective celebration of socially significant lives is something which does not feature.

It sometimes amazes me that when you read the story of Jesus, the only named people of any national standing with whom he engages are Herod and Pontius Pilate ... both of whom appear in a negative light.

The named people – the people the Gospel hurls into public discourse for two thousand years – are Martha, a home-maker, and Simon, a firebrand, and James and John who were argumentative brothers, and Joanna and Susanna, wives of civil servants; and a host of women called Mary known some for virtue, some for vice.

And these ... not the sporting heroes, not the distinguished actors and infamous drama queens; these ... not the people whose latest purchases or peccadilloes were the stuff of society gossip ... these nobodies were the people who fascinated God enough that he came in Jesus to call them his friends.

30 Dec 2003

Treasure chest or empty box

... in defence of the forgotten potential in remembering

Wee, sleekit, cow'rin' tim'rous beastie,
oh, what a panic's on thy breastie!
Thou need na start awa' sae hasty
wi' bick'rin brattle ...

... I don't think that was the one she remembered. How about:
I wandered lonely as a cloud
that floats on high o'er vales and hills?

No. I don't think that was the one she remembered either.

In fact I'm certain, because the poem she remembered would probably have been in Arabic. And she ... the mysterious literary figure ... she ... is Shahrbanou Mazandarani, and she's 98 years old. She's the woman who was discovered in the ruined Iranian city of Bann, alive and in good shape, eight days after the earthquake.

She was found to be reciting poetry, a practice which – along with her faith – helped to keep her alive. She is a singular witness to that great untapped resource of memory which the Western world so often devalues.

Oh yes, we have plenty of competitions and game shows in which contestants empty the contents of their brains by responding to such deeply intriguing questions as:
When did Accrington Stanley last win the FA cup? or
When was the last year that Tomintoul was not cut off by snow?

But as a reservoir of resources for living, rather than a depository of facts, the memory is often neglected.

Not so in Africa. I have a friend, George Mxadana, who conducts a choir in Soweto. When he told me that his choir sang the Messiah I asked him which version they used. 'Version?' he responded. 'We sing from memory ... everything, always from memory. Unless it is held deeply inside us we will not communicate.'

That same facility is present in Muslims who can recite large portions of the Koran, and it was evident in the Celtic monks who – like the rabbis of Jesus' day – could repeat the whole book of Psalms by heart.

But let me go back to Shahrbanou Mazandarani and her ability to recite poems while buried from human view for a week. It makes me wonder what those of us who live frenetic lives would do were we buried under rubble for that length of time, unable to be distracted by background muzak or inane chatter. Is there anything deeply etched or embedded in our memories that would sustain us? ... anything from which we could draw encouragement or even prepare to meet our maker?

Perhaps it is not outer space or the ocean bed that is the last untapped resource. Perhaps it is our own ability to remember the things which, in more desperate days, might nourish us.

6 Jan 04

A parental quandary

... re what to pray if your son is gay

I had an interesting conversation recently with a high court judge from South Africa.

He was firmly of the belief that former proponents of apartheid should be held accountable for the high incidence of HIV/AIDS which affects up to one in four people in some South African communities.

Previous governments prevented people who loved each other from living together. Laws against interracial marriage kept some apart, while others were caught up in the migrant labour market.

This required men to leave their homes and families for months on end, and to live in compounds hundreds of miles away next to gold or diamond mines. Being separated from their partners for long periods of time, the temptation to infidelity was too much for many. They slept around, became infected and then passed on the virus to their spouses and – through the womb – to their children.

Under the respectable mantles of public decency and economic necessity, promiscuity and its inherent dangers were encouraged.

I was thinking about this the other day when I read about how in San Francisco the mayor is wilfully flouting state law by issuing marriage licences to gay couples.

This may upset or offend some of us, but let's leave our gut feelings aside for a moment. Imagine you have a son of 21 who is witty, athletic, handsome, kind ... and he brings home a girl he has been going out with. You see from the light in his eyes and in hers that this is a good relationship. It looks as if it will last and you hope and pray that it will develop into marriage, blissful intimacy and children.

Imagine you have another son, equally attractive, handsome, gregarious and kind. But instead of bringing a girl home, he tells you he is gay. What do you wish for him – lifelong singleness, no knowledge of physical intimacy, but perhaps a passion for books or religion which will compensate? And if he must exercise his sexuality, then pray God let no one know about it.

Might it be that in encouraging a committed relationship in the one, but denying it to the other we actually encourage promiscuity and its consequences, in the same way as Afrikaaners with their high moral and religious principles encouraged AIDS?

God, according to the Bible, reckoned that it was not good for individuals to be alone. That divine perspective is echoed at countless marriages where these words from the Bible are read:

Where you go I will go
and where you live I will live.
Your people will be my people
and your God my God.

How odd that these words were not first said by a bride to her groom, but by one woman to another.

19 Feb 04

lent

A season to prove who is in charge

... being one of the by-products of Lent

It's always at this time of year that I remember a friend of mine who used to be a theatre musician. He decided that for Lent he would give up drinking tea and coffee. Two weeks into his abstinent regime, I asked him how he was doing.

'Not bad,' he replied, 'except that I've had to take caffeine tablets to keep me awake in the orchestra pit.'

The practice of giving up something for Lent – the season of penitence which began yesterday – has in recent years been played down. The new wisdom is that we should take something up – visit people who are lonely, read a serious book.

I would not disparage that for a moment, but neither would I want to discourage abstinence, albeit temporary. And a plethora of surveys on obesity and diet, culminating in a recent report about public health debated yesterday on the *Today* programme, encourages me to reconsider the value of giving certain things up for Lent.

As with many devotional exercises, refraining voluntarily from certain patterns of behaviour reaps both spiritual and physical benefits – especially in the context of a faith which believes that bodies are important as well as souls.

The spiritual benefit has to do with how relationships require sacrifice. If you are going to get married, you cannot expect to pursue exactly the same lifestyle as you did as a single person. Some pastimes, some indulgences, have to be sacrificed as a sign of love and to deepen that love. You cannot experience marital bliss if you persist in acting as if you were the unhitched bachelor boy or girl.

And if a relationship with God is to count rather than be a casual affair, there have to be deliberate decisions as regards the use of time, money and prayer which will consolidate the relationship and affirm its worth.

But I said that giving up particular habits or pleasures was good for the body as well as the soul. Of course it is. It shows who is in charge.

Is my fondness for fast food in charge of me, or am I in charge of it?

Is my urge to buy new clothes every week a sign of fashion consciousness or of personal discontent?

Is my need always to have two or three drinks with a meal a real threat to my health which I interpret as being sociable?

Is filling every hour of the day with business actually a means of avoiding having to deal with my marriage or my children or myself?

Perhaps the term 'nanny state' would not have to be used with regard to government intervention in matters of personal health and welfare if more of us were able to take charge of our lifestyles rather than plead that we are the helpless victims of consumer choice.

This season gives us that opportunity. Happy Lent.

26 Feb 04

A necessary virtue
for a potential president

... not that everyone would agree

They'll have heard about it in Chad, and they'll be reading about it in East Timor.

And it would be hard to imagine a meeting of teachers, lawyers or financiers in Kabul, Helsinki, Budapest or Manila where it will not be a topic of conversation.

And many of us learned about it yesterday on the *Today* programme, but can do little about it though it might affect all of us.

I am referring, of course, to the emergence of John Kerry as the preferred Democratic candidate for the American presidential elections, not due to be held until November.

There is an odd irony that despite the USA having a lower turn-out at the polls than many countries it has lectured about democracy, the appearance of a presidential *candidate* is world news six months before election day.

But then, this election – undoubtedly the most expensive in history, as always – is about choosing the most powerful man in the world.

That being the case and American foreign policy and American corporate interests having an undoubted global impact, shouldn't the rest of the world have a say in the contest? I mean, if nations like Chile and Nicaragua and Haiti have had their choice of their political masters influenced by the USA, is there no reciprocal agreement?

Or, failing that, couldn't the United Nations on behalf of the world community come to a consensus as to which candidate's policy would be most beneficial to global security, the eradication of poverty, and the protection of the environment?

Being put in a position of unparalleled terrestrial power without having any international accountability is probably the nearest thing we have to playing God. And if an individual aspires to such an office, perhaps he should be judged according to what divine attributes he shows.

What would these attributes be? What are the attributes of God which a man who rules the world by proxy should have?

A wide knowledge of human nature and international affairs? ... yes.

An ability to command respect and exercise power? ... certainly.

A total integrity of thought and action? ... of course.

But I would plead for one other attribute – the ability to change his mind.

To Christians as much as to non-believers or other believers, this may seem anathema. But for the God of the Bible, this is a quintessential attribute – the ability to change mind and change actions when justice and compassion demand it.

That's what makes a truly great leader.

4 Mar 04

That without which our humanity withers

... an observation on the response to a disaster

It's an odd thing to turn on the television and see a live picture of the street on which you live. But when you realise that it is not a celebrity who has been spotted but a disaster which is being reported, any thrill or excitement soon evaporates. And that is what has happened as 500 yards from where I live firefighters are trying to rescue people whose workplace was destroyed around them by an explosion.

Maryhill Road is a silent place. Normally it would resound to children playing, shoppers coming out of a nearby supermarket and the occasional drunk man celebrating or bemoaning the fate of Partick Thistle.

In some ways the complex operation to rescue people trapped in the collapsed factory has been of textbook quality. The emergency response systems worked well.

But it is not satisfaction you see on the faces of the rescue staff. Nor is it boredom, even though there have been long times of waiting. The mood – if one could call it that – has been one of dignity – which is perhaps the most appropriate gift to offer to those who are injured or anxious or broken.

Dignity ... as when tough men tenderly comforted each other when they realised how close they had come to losing each other.

Dignity ... as when fire and police chiefs dealt only with fact and eschewed sensational speculation.

Dignity ... in the way rescuers handled the dead in body bags as carefully as they carried the living.

Such dignity. It would have warmed the heart of Wole Soyinka, the Nigerian writer and Nobel prize-winner. A fortnight ago, in the Reith lectures, he lamented the absence of that quality where it is most needed.

Dignity – evident in Maryhill this week, but less so in the treatment of captives whether in Iraqi prisons or British jails. And not always evident in the way we suspect rather than respect the strangers who live among us.

Wole Soyinka's claim was that only human beings can rob the dignity from others. It's not the camera which vilifies Iraqi prisoners; it's the photographer. It's not exile which demeans asylum-seekers; it's the persecutors in their home country and the staring neighbours in their host community.

So now I understand why I am moved by the story of Jesus kneeling beside a woman who was about to be stoned. He was letting his dignity bend low to restore hers.

And now I know why I admire the women who tend the dead Christ at the foot of the cross. Like the police and ambulance staff and rescuers in Maryhill, they revere rather than degrade the human face of God.

14 May 04

prophecy

Peripheral vision

... as possessed by true prophets

The other day I was on the phone to an American college student at whose graduation a Republican Senator was extolling the virtues of the Iraq war.

'Did he say that he had stopped reading the papers, like Donald Rumsfeld?' I asked. Andrew, the student, a worldly aware Democrat, was puzzled by this allusion to what the US Defence Secretary had said recently on his surprise visit to Baghdad. 'I don't think we've heard about that here,' he replied.

'So, if the news doesn't tell you the news,' I asked, 'who does?'

And then I suppose I must have sounded like my grandfather as I alluded to how during the Vietnam War and its aftermath there were singers like Bob Dylan and Joan Baez who, in popular culture, protested against the war and debunked the myths of Western superiority.

'I don't think we've anyone like that at the moment,' he replied, 'except Bono, who we've imported from Ireland, and maybe Michael Moore.'

Now there's a force to be reckoned with,

Michael Moore is the film producer whose most recent production, *Fahrenheit 9/11*, has been applauded at Cannes, but is the subject of cinematographic intrigue in the USA. It seems that Disney, which controls the distribution rights, doesn't want to handle a film which might compromise its privileged position *vis à vis* Jeb Bush, the president's brother and the governor of Florida.

That, for me at least, suggests that there might be something of the prophet in Moore.

Normally the word prophet is associated with names like Mohammed, Jeremiah or – for new age enthusiasts – Kahlil Gibran.

In the biblical tradition, a prophet is not a fortune-teller, but someone who sees the bigger picture which the national leadership is avoiding, someone whose loyalty – not hatred but loyalty – to his or her nation leads to perceptions that may be at odds with current political wisdom; someone who believes that things can change and who, for his or her efforts, may be labelled subversive, eccentric or deranged.

Whether or not Moore can lay claim to the prophet's mantle may be disputed. He has, after all, a personal agenda to unseat the president. But in an era when popular music and the populist media have more to do with hedonism than altruism, it is surely important that there are people not in the pay of any political party who offer alternative perspectives.

I suggest this because the witness of the Bible is that the centre can only get it right when the periphery is providing a vision.

21 May 2004

transport

The best of the West
... an everyday story of city folk

Let me introduce you to the Wests.

Perhaps I should say the 'very' Wests, for George and Fiona live in Westfield Drive in the West End of Glasgow.

She is a part-time solicitor working in the city; he is the regional director of a company based in Manchester. They have three children, the youngest of whom, Sarah, is still at school; and they have three cars – one for him, one for her and one for whichever of the older offspring needs wheels.

Sarah gets run into school each day. She could go on the bus, but her parents prefer the personal touch, even though she's sixteen. Her mum drives into the city centre in the afternoon. She could take the train, but that would mean walking about 500 yards to and from the station and sometimes it rains. George flies to Manchester once a week. He also could take the train, but if the company is paying, why not fly?

This week has seen the Wests get hot under the collar about the price of petrol. George thinks that 83 pence per litre is extortionate. He says they can't afford it, especially as two of their cars do only 27 miles to the gallon.

Fiona was more alarmed about a news report the other evening which said that in the past year car ownership in Shanghai had risen by 60%. She can't understand why a previously rural economy which has done very well with rickshaws should suddenly want to get motorised with all the noise and pollution that accompanies it. 'I don't want Shanghai to end up like Great Western Road on a school morning,' she said.

The Wests are very devout people. So they both felt independently that they should pray about what others are calling the fuel crisis. But what to pray? There's the rub.

Should they ask God to persuade those two nice Scotsmen in the cabinet, Mr Brown and Mr Darling, to defer any increase in petrol tax? Should they ask God to make Saudi Arabia safe so that the threat of terrorism won't raise the price of oil? Or should they ask God to preserve indigenous Chinese culture?

Poor old God. Their prayers threatened to sound like a multiple choice question in an economics A level.

As it happened, they didn't ask for any of these things.

They opened their eyes and Fiona said, 'It's time Sarah walked to school, and I'll take the bus to the office. There's one every 10 minutes.'

And George said, 'I'm going to take the train to Manchester. It's more eco-friendly and the journey is about to get quicker.'

Together they shouted, 'Let's get rid of two of the cars!'

And they hugged each other and booked a meal at the Ping Shang Chinese restaurant to celebrate their decisions.

That's a nice story, isn't it? – though God didn't have much to do in it, except encourage people in the West to take responsibility for the earth ... which at the moment is a big part of God's job.

28 May 04

Old-style education

... on a day when good results are marked down

I have just come back from working in one country where churches run a summer education programme in English and maths for pupils whom the state system is failing, and another country where state schooling doesn't begin until children are seven years old.

The first country is the USA and the second Romania, and the shortcomings of both put into context the denigration of the British educational system which seems *de rigueur* at the moment.

On a day on which A level results are being delivered or opened as I speak, what encouragement must it be to pupils – never mind teachers – to hear accusations that standards must have slipped because too many pupils are achieving high grades?

There is not a finite pool of intelligence to which only a minority may lay claim.

It's a bit like saying that a fringe show in the current Edinburgh Festival should have a certain quota of laughs and if more people laugh than is expected, it proves that the entertainment must be of an inferior quality.

There is a recurrent injunction that runs through the Hebrew and Christian scriptures which is apposite for this issue. It is the command to remember – sometimes to remember your Maker, sometimes to remember your pedigree, sometimes to remember your personal life-journey, sometimes to remember your nation's history. And God encourages such remembering, because God knows that human beings are prone to selective forgetting. When that happens, subjectivity becomes the sole perspective for assessing major issues; and major issues need to be discussed in a broader context.

As one whose school qualifications would not now get me anywhere near a university, I can hardly substantiate the claim that standards have fallen.

I and others may bemoan a lack of discipline in some schools, but do we want to go back even to forty years ago when left-handed pupils, of whom my brother was one, were compelled to use their right? And have I forgotten how we had teachers who physically belted nine-year-olds for misspelling more than three words out of ten? ... or how in the high school we had a classics master who delighted in administering corporal punishment to sixth-form girls?

Do we want to go back to the days when it was seen as a virtue to be able to recite from memory the names of the books of the Bible, but nothing was said about the Koran except by way of disparagement?

Do we want to go back to the days when, at the age of 11, a line was drawn between an egalitarian childhood education and an adolescent schooling which encouraged elitism, social disintegration and a denial of opportunity to late developers?

We do well to remember how these very vices thrived in the good old days when a small minority took A levels. But now that the old seedbeds have gone, we should be glad that there is more and better fruit.

19 Aug 04

Not driving on neutral

... in sport or religion

The other day at the Edinburgh Film Festival, there was the British premier of a Chilean film which, among other things, proved that sport is not neutral. The film, *Machucha*, is set in 1973 when the democratically elected government of Salvador Allende was overthrown by General Pinochet.

There's a brief scene after the coup in which a man on a bus is reading a newspaper with the headlines
    'FIFA SAYS CHILE IS CLEAR'.

The reference is to how the Russian national football team refused to play in Chile's national stadium because it was allegedly a place of torture and internment. FIFA (the international football authority) investigated and gave the stadium the all-clear.

What FIFA did not know was that its investigators had been hoodwinked. The stadium had been cleared of internees just for their visit. The resulting clean bill of health helped to improve Pinochet's credibility.

This may ring bells with those who are following the dispute as to whether George Bush should or should not visit Athens. On his campaign trail he has made great issue of Iraq and Afghanistan competing at the Olympics thanks to their liberation. But Iraqi and Afghani athletes do not want either these comments or his appearance at the games to be credibility fodder for his re-election.

Sport cannot be indifferent. Of that I'm glad, because it makes a good bedfellow with that other pastime for some and passion for others which is religion. Those who claim that religion is or should be a neutral thing simply have no grasp on reality past or present.

In the 1980s Southern Baptist congregations took offerings in church to help the contras overthrow Ortega in Nicaragua. And recently certain Roman Catholic bishops in the United States have expressed a reticence to let John Kerry receive holy communion because he is pro-choice.

I could just as easily speak of Christians whose words and actions have been as liberating as these examples were restricting. Indeed, the film *Machucha* alludes to a real priest who was imprisoned because he stood up for the poor against Pinochet.

The issue is that, as with sport, there are those who claim that their passion is divorced from their politics. And there are others who, right wing or left wing, admit that their faith affects their life choices.

And I prefer the latter, because any system of belief which claims that God made the world, but that faith in God should not influence its politics, is not faith but escapism.

If you love what God cherishes, you can't be neutral.

26 Aug 04

A partiality for justice

... as a prerequisite for sitting on the Bench

I once asked a member of the judiciary whether judges were impartial.

'No,' he replied. 'It's impossible.'

And then he continued: 'Look at me. I grew up with a silver spoon in my mouth. I had a privileged education. I have never wanted for anything and I've always been surrounded by successful, affluent white people.

'What am I to do when a black woman appears in front of me about whom all I know is that she stole food from a supermarket. She has broken the law and for such a transgression the law requires a punishment.

'What do I know about the poverty, alienation and possible abuse which has required her to steal in order to feed her family?'

My respondent was not a weekend magistrate, but a High Court judge in a place where politics once compromised the administration of justice. He is Johan Kreigler of South Africa, the man who was entrusted with the oversight of that country's first democratic elections.

Though in his retirement years, he has not withdrawn from making the processes of law more equitable, but spends a lot of time enabling black, coloured and other minority barristers to learn from his experience so that they may be better prepared for elevation to the Bench.

So, it's good to hear that Britain is considering following South Africa's example as regards ethnic minorities and women, the more so when one considers how half of those who qualify as barristers are women, but only a sixth of judges are female.

But is it the case – as some would fear – that there's a danger of black judges being more sympathetic to black defendants, and female judges being more sympathetic to thieving housewives? ... as if affluent white judges would never be biased in favour of defendants from their own class.

No. The issue, to use a biblical term, is to ensure that judges, like God, judge with justice. And this is not simply a matter of concluding whether or not a crime has been committed. It's to do with understanding the context of the crime, having some grasp of the social or psychological pressures on the offender, assessing what is the most appropriate punishment and last, but by no means least, adding to the collective wisdom of the justiciary.

And this cannot happen if the majority of judges have been reared and educated in a fashion common only to the more privileged echelons in society.

Judging with justice has as much to do with insight as it has to do with recognising criminality.

... all of which makes me wonder whether the course of history might have been very different if Jesus' fate had been decreed not by Pilate who feared his political paymasters, but by Pilate's wife who, given the same evidence, was convinced that Jesus was innocent.

14 Oct 04

gambling

The proposed enthronement
of an old pretender

... coming, perhaps, to a town near you

Did you know that Las Vegas is a favourite holiday destination for American Roman Catholic nuns? It's not that the sisters have secret addictions. It's simply that big hotels in Las Vegas are cheap.

I discovered this when I was at a liturgical musicians' conference.

I also discovered that the favourite key of casino owners is C.

It was a man with perfect pitch who pointed this out as we walked through the caverns of one-armed bandits that you can't avoid. He said, 'Listen to the notes ringing out whenever someone pulls a lever.' Sure enough, there was the tonic chord of C major permeating the tinkle of quarters and dimes as they entered and exited the machines.

And the reason? It had been discovered that a C major chord in whatever constellation has a relaxing effect on punters.

Equally disorienting is the seeming absence of time.

The gaming halls are like heaven. They give the impression of endless day and endless dining. With no windows to look out and restaurants serving suppers and breakfasts simultaneously, it is hard for the inveterate or casual gambler to know whether it is night or morning.

And all this ... all this and so much more could be ours, if parliament will only assent to a bill which, under the guise of regulating gambling, will enable financial predators to erect twenty mega casinos (or is it forty or might it be more?) on British shores.

The comparison with Las Vegas is a bit spurious. People go there because the 24-hour gambling and entertainment ethos is unique. For some punters, it's only while on a holiday in that resort that they play for big stakes. For the rest of the time, putting their name on the stub of a raffle-ticket might be their only other engagement with games of chance.

But what might happen if a quasi- or semi-Las Vegas experience were offered as a year-round feature of life in Hull or Caernarvon or Londonderry or Fort William? (I choose these places because out-of-season entertainment might be a boost to the local economy.)

Some Christians object to gambling on the basis that games of chance can be addictive to vulnerable people and that such a diversion of money can cause personal and family ruin.

Personally I think it has also to do with idolatry. What ultimately do we serve and in whom do we put our trust? The bitch goddess Lady Luck may be the pretender to the throne of human hearts. There is no need to make her queen.

Avarice – both personal and corporate – is an activity which all humanitarians discourage. Why, then, should we institutionalise it?

21 Oct 04

Israel

Soundbites are for the short haul
... when the bigger picture needs attention

Sub specie aeternitatis ... I'll say that again
Sub specie aeternitatis ... is not as popular as it once was.

There are two reasons. One is that Latin has long since stopped being the lingua franca. The other is that the sentiment is not in vogue.

Sub specie aeternitatis means: in the context of eternity. It has to do with the bigger picture rather than the distracting detail, the long haul rather than gesture politics.

And it came to mind yesterday when I was thinking about Ariel Sharon, that old Jewish war-horse, patriot of Israel, scourge of the Palestinians and now, it seems, political turncoat. For, though being one of the main proponents of the settlements, Sharon engineered what he called 'a fateful moment for Israel' in getting a majority of the Knesset to favour the withdrawal of settlers from Gaza and part of the West Bank.

Did some Arab slip him an envelope? Is this the first sign of senility? Or is it that having led the battle for so long, he has sensed the futility of the war, and realises that, in the long-term interests of the Israelis, Palestinians and their land-rights have to be accommodated?

Sharon comes from a country which was forged around words that spoke of the need for a sense of perspective ...

... words from the Psalms like:
> *Lord, let us know the number of our days*
> *that our minds may learn wisdom.*

... or again
> *In your sight, a thousand years*
> *are like a passing day.*

This acknowledgement of a bigger context in which decisions need to be made runs counter to a sound-bite culture. As politicians ably demonstrate on this programme, the rapid recitation of statistics can become a diversion from the underlying complex or deeper issues.

Is our primary concern to increase medical provision for the sick – or to identify and combat unhealthy lifestyles which make people ill?

Is the building of more prisons a substitute for tackling the systemic roots of crime, particularly in disadvantaged communities?

Is the maintenance of America's status as the world's only super-power in the long-term interest of the other 93% of humanity?

Elections and popularity may be won by talking up instant and attractive solutions to intractable problems, but the radical thing is to look at the root cause rather than the thermometer of popular opinion.

That is why any religion or any politics which deals primarily with quick fixes and easy answers must be suspected. We may prefer *ad hominem*. God favours *sub specie aeternitatis*.

28 Oct 04

The school nativity play

... an objective account

We tend to think that Christmas is a time for children. That's why we get them to do nativity plays. But do they learn the story? Here's one child's testimony:

'Christmas is a time for children because the baby Jesus was a child. So were his mum and dad. Mary was ten when she had her baby, because that's how old Sheryl Foster is, and Joseph was eleven like Ravinder Singh.

'Joseph was not the real daddy of Jesus. The real daddy was Mr Montgomery, our school janitor, who is also Santa Claus.

'Mary was pregnant, but stayed very thin, unlike my mum when she was having wee Sandra. Mary always wore a blue nightie, and Joseph wore a dressing gown like Ravinder Singh's dad.

'Mary and Joseph had to travel from the back of the school hall to Bethlehem on a donkey called Gerry after Mr Montgomery the janitor.

'Caesar Augustus wanted the whole world to be taxed. That is why everybody went to Bethlehem and it was so crowded. People had even come from Africa and Australia because there is no snow there.

'Mary decided that she was going to have the baby right away in the snow because there was no room at the Inn. The innkeeper had a wife whose name was Veronica. She was also one of the ugly sisters with big feet.

'The innkeeper's name was Lo, because Joseph said to him, *Lo, my wife is great with child.*

'Lo took Mary and Joseph to a dirty cowshed. It was full of steam and smells from the pigs and cows and hens who had gathered together for the census.

'Mary had her baby in front of everybody. When he arrived everybody realised why she was dressed in blue. She knew it was going to be a boy. She called him Jesus and immediately he sat up and pointed to the roof where there was a draught.

'Some shepherds came to see the baby. They had been told by the angels to bring a lamb. Joseph put it in the manger beside the baby Jesus.

'The shepherds got in just before the wise men who wore Mrs Anderson's silk scarves after they promised not to wipe their nose on them.

'The wise men had gifts for the baby – a big stone covered with gold paper, a perfume bottle full of cochineal and incense sticks. Joseph put these in the manger next to the lamb and the baby Jesus.

'Then the shepherds and the wise men knelt down in front of the baby Jesus and sang *Jingle Bells*. Then Mr Montgomery came in dressed as Santa Claus. But Mrs Anderson shouted at him because it was not time yet.'

If you find this funny, Happy Christmas. If you're offended, stop asking children to do the nativity play. It's really a story for adults.

23 Dec 04

Help or hedonism

... or how junk mail hinders generosity

Yesterday I opened the box, but tomorrow I will empty it.

It was a New Year's resolution last year: to keep all unsolicited mail in one container. It now weighs about half a stone ... only a fraction of what I would weigh had I indulged in the countless Mexican Pizza, Indian Curry, Mediterranean Kebab bargains which arrive via the letterbox at the rate of two per week.

Still, there was also a cut price offer to a slimming club – but that was only for women, and I don't look good in drag.

I discovered that a number of finance houses had preselected me for bargain car insurance – which is interesting, given that I don't drive; and looking through the telephone deals was like watching a badminton match with BT on the one side and everyone else on the other.

I regret that I never opened any of the ten envelopes which announced that I had won a major prize in a draw I never entered. I may have missed winning up to £60,000 several times over, plus holidays in the Bahamas and a gold-tapped jacuzzi.

Still, if I want to purchase what I forfeited – including the Mexican pizzas – I have loan offers which total over a quarter of a million pounds from eight different banks

And as if that is not enough, there are, in the box, eleven

credit cards-in-waiting – both platinum and gold. All that's needed is my signature and an unspecified amount of financial freedom could be mine courtesy of five different counting houses.

Tomorrow I'm going to empty the box and I won't resolve to fill it again with another year's junk mail, none of which – incidentally – is printed on recycled paper.

But seeing it all together has been a good exercise. If it has one thread in common it is consumption – the consumption of food, petrol, tourism, home improvements, insurance to safeguard what I've bought, and debt to pay for what I've been seduced into needing.

'And what has all this to do with the tsunami disaster?' I hear someone asking. Nothing ... absolutely nothing, except that it throws into contrast what life is ultimately about.

Is the purpose of our being here to inoculate ourselves from reality by indulging our ever-present hedonistic tendencies, or is it to develop our altruistic potential?

Take the phrase in the Lord's Prayer 'Your kingdom come'. Is that fulfilled through junk mail or in generosity, in wanting what we don't have or in giving to people who have lost everything?

The world will not be changed next year when the G8 leaders meet in the hermetically sealed environment of Gleneagles Hotel, but when we – the affluent – let God's kingdom come by forsaking the junk mail and embracing generosity and justice.

30 Dec 04

Owning up to our responsibilities
... as regards aid and trade

Every weekday in Glasgow, you can scarcely walk along Sauchiehall Street without being confronted with animated twenty-year-old interviewers dressed in fluorescent jackets.

They are employed by a number of the larger charities to raise funds. I feel very ambivalent towards them because I think that it's unfair that the big fish are allowed to dominate the limited pool of benevolence, while smaller charities are sidelined.

So, the issue arose for me whether to warm to Bob Geldof's recently announced Live 8 extravaganza or – as some critics suggest – to see it as little more than an exercise in self-publicity for ageing rock-stars, a displacement activity which will detract from the real issues.

And that was the attitude I was tempted to espouse until I realised two things.

The first is that given the choice of the rock glitterati being celebrated for their sex lives or for their altruism, I would go for the latter. Compared to the sixties and seventies, there are few high-profile popular musicians who associate either their lyrics or themselves with issues of social and international justice. If such people can have influence, then let it be egalitarian rather than egocentric.

But the second thing I realised was that Live 8 is not primarily a money-raising venture which might siphon funds away from other worthy causes.

Live 8 and the Campaign to Make Poverty History are about influencing political decision-making, asking the Western nations to take responsibility for the effect their economic, trade, and self-benefiting aid policies have had on the world's poorest.

As long as Ghanaian farmers cannot compete with subsidised rice from the USA and Europe, can we be indifferent?

As long as HIV-infected women throughout sub-Saharan Africa cannot get the promised retrovirals because of EU red tape, can we be neutral??

As long as impoverished countries like Angola are suddenly courted by Western banks because oil has been discovered which we need to maintain our levels of consumption, can we claim innocence?

... and as long as these things coexist with high-level corruption sometimes endorsed by the West, then concerned people have to use every means they can to put such gross violations of humanity on the agenda of the politicians who have the power to effect change.

My understanding of the day of judgement is increasingly less about God taking out a black book to remind individuals of the wrong they did, and more about God – in the fashion of one of Jesus' parables – asking nations ... *nations* ... why they failed to protect and to prosper the poor.

2 June 05

The deception of self-perception

... when it comes to social and international justice

There's an often misquoted line by my fellow countryman, Robert Burns:

O wad some Power the giftie gie us
tae see oorsels as ithers see us.

The 'giftie' (meaning small gift) is an understanding of how we appear in other people's eyes.

I remember this 'giftie' being given me in Holland where I heard people referring to the 'civil war' Britain was encouraging in Northern Ireland. I was offended. It was a sectarian skirmish according to my lights, but not according to outside observers.

And I was, in a way, wishing that 'giftie' on the USA yesterday when I heard President Bush saying that Americans were world leaders in action on global warming – a sentiment which must appal the world's science academies which regard the American government as a pariah when it comes to concern for climate control.

But any gloating on America's inability to appreciate how it is viewed elsewhere was quickly dissipated when the news came out as to how Álvaro Gil-Robles, the European Human Rights Commissioner, views our criminal justice system, particularly as regards the treatment of prisoners and asylum-seekers, and the issuing of Control Orders.

To discover that this civilised nation, which prides itself in justice for all, should be found wanting by an outsider is a little unsettling to say the least.

Is it that Mr Gil-Robles has simply failed to understand the United Kingdom? Is it that his research is too limited? Or is our annoyance rooted in a defensiveness that wants to assert, in the face of the facts, that it is the rest of the world which is out of step?

It happened that just before the Human Rights Commissioner's comments were made public, I had been in a discussion about the penal system and our treatment or rather containment of offenders. We were trying to understand what Jesus meant when he said that he had come to set the captives free. Did that mean that all jails should be emptied in the name of God?

And then one woman suggested that the captivity which cries out for release may be that mentality which sees every criminal as an irredeemable wrongdoer, every asylum-seeker as a social parasite and every Muslim who expresses discontent with the West as a potential terrorist.

Jesus, who was very good at one-liners, once said to a group his self-righteous compatriots,
    'Because you claim to see, your guilt remains.'

Maybe in that light it would do us good to value the 'giftie' of how other people perceive us.

9 June 05

Invented or reported?

... a comment on the news

When I heard yesterday that Rupert Murdoch was going to give a reading at the farewell-to-Fleet-Street service at St Bride's Church, I began to speculate on what might be appropriate texts for the great man to read.

I wondered if Galatians 1 verse 23 might epitomise the transfer of political allegiance of the Murdoch Press in favour of the Labour Party:

Our former persecutor is now preaching the good news.

Or, considering ongoing tabloid rivalry, the Sun's editorial department might find itself represented in a verse from St Matthew's Gospel:

And when they saw the Star, they went home by another way.

But given the shared affection of many national dailies for the human anatomy, an appropriate In Memoriam for Fleet Street might include lines from the Song of Songs such as:

I have taken off my robe.
Must I put it on again?

As it happened, Brother Rupert read the familiar passage from Ecclesiasticus which begins, 'Let us now praise famous men.'

Still I suppose if I could choose one text which would relate to journalism, it would be the question which Pilate asks Jesus before pronouncing sentence:

What is truth?
... for that's surely the issue we all grapple with in trying to differentiate between what's fact and what's fiction.

If a columnist writes,
> 'As yet the prime minister has not denied that he has some carefully concealed tattoos'

... is the writer telling the truth or starting a rumour?

If another 'exclusively reveals' that ...
> 'Several Tory backbenchers are said to be concerned that none of the rumoured leadership candidates is a left-handed vegetarian'

... who is going to refute this invention before it becomes headline news?

These ... of course ... are hypothetical examples. But as regards recent news, whether it be the aftermath of the Michael Jackson trial or the dissension regarding the EU budget, the slant or bias of a journalist will either accurately reflect or eclipse the truth.

You cannot divorce the message from the messenger. But as Rowan Williams suggested in a lecture last night, it's quite reasonable in a civilised society to expect reporters to nourish the common good by differentiating between information and speculation.

That is maybe what concerns Pilate. He is confronted with someone whose primary intention is not to distort reality but to reveal the truth. And in Pilate's experience – as in ours – the facts are sometimes more of a threat than the fiction. So we – and he – go for gossip rather than accuracy ... or is that just a matter of opinion?

16 June 05

alcohol

A plea for fewer cheers
... in the best interests of the bottoms-up brigade

What do you think would happen if it were discovered that 50% of the prison population in Britain had been helped on the road to crime because of one identifiable food additive which had an adverse effect on behaviour?

There would be a public outcry. There would be demands that this ingredient be banned. And if the malign propensities of this food additive had been common knowledge for some time, government ministers would be pilloried for not acting sooner.

So why do beer glasses not have a sign which states:
'Alcohol may lead to criminal activity of a violent nature, dangerous driving and lasting damage to the health of the liver.'

Why do beer glasses not say that? And why do bottles of alcohol not carry a government health warning at least as evident as that on cigarette packets?

This is not a plea for total abstinence. I respect that position, but I don't regard it as a Christian absolute, especially since one of the biblical images of heaven is of a great feast with good food, fine wine and no hangovers.

But I've been alarmed recently by published statistics regarding alcohol-related crime. Then yesterday came news of a running battle three hundred drunken football supporters had with the Newcastle police on Sunday night.

And at the weekend, the head of the National Association of Licensed House Managers talked of how companies which own chains of pubs – the very people who have been lobbying for extended drinking hours – these same companies have been offering bonuses of up to £20,000 per year to bar managers to encourage binge drinking, effectively turning public houses into freestyle communal vomitariums.

The sought-after extension of hours is supposed to bring us into line with the continent – though I'd imagine many of the suppliants for this cause are probably eurosceptic on other matters of continental polity.

Why not move into line with Australia where, in some states, bar staff are required to stop serving drunken customers, and pubs have to ensure that those who leave the premises late at night keep their noise level down within a 300-metre radius.

Two of the less respectable epithets used of Jesus referred to him as a glutton and a drunkard. You don't attract that kind of name-calling by sticking to bread and water.

Jesus both enjoyed and encouraged hospitality ... in order that people might become more fully themselves. Drunkenness makes people less fully themselves and it inevitably exacerbates that part of themselves they can't cope with when they are sober. No humane society should use extended hours or happy hours to encourage that kind of displacement activity.

25 Oct 05

The French Foreign Legion
... or the multiple causes of social disorder

When I was 19, I read a book which made an indelible impression on me. The title I forget, but the subject I remember. It was geriatric medicine. And the central thesis was that a body is never affected by a generic thing called old age, but rather by a combination of disorders – some physical, some psychological, some social. When they are individually recognised and treated, the health of the body can be repaired.

Among other things, this analysis helped me to understand a line in the Bible which had always puzzled me. It's the response that Jesus gets when he asks the name of the evil spirit dementing a sick man.

'Our name is legion,' is the reply, 'for there are many of us.' Madness – like old age, is not a single-issue illness.

What is true for the body physical is sometimes also true for the body politic. A social disorder which manifests itself in one sector of the population may encourage ill-informed condemnation from another. Thus employed people end up calling unemployed people work-shy, or self-made entrepreneurs accuse those on the minimum wage of being lazy.

Often, the social malaise (singular) is something much more complex ... as is increasingly evident in the country from which the term *malaise* comes.

What seemed to be a purely Parisian affair – rioting in the streets, destruction of property, torching of vehicles – has become a national phenomenon, with previously stable cities like Toulouse being affected.

The response of the interior minister, Nicolas Sarkozy, calling the rioters 'scum' and 'yobs' has only exacerbated the situation, and brought into the fray people who had hitherto been passive spectators.

There is no one disorder, there are many. The rioters are mainly but not exclusively black North Africans, who like British Muslims have been sensitised to institutional racism. They are also young, and may be experiencing what many second-generation immigrants feel – a disaffection with the country their parents chose to settle in, married to a frustration of being unable to become the native Africans or Arabs they wish they were.

On top of this, many of the disaffected youth live in areas where up to 40% of the population is under 25, and up to 40% of 25-year-olds are unemployed.

What is the name of this disorder? The name is Legion for they are many … which means that for France, as for any European country that has estranged ethnic communities living in impoverished neighbourhoods, simple solutions are as deficient as branding every dissident a yob or scum.

France has to find not one remedy but a variety of responses. For it is affected not by an illness (singular) but by malaises (plural).

8 Nov 05

Celtic connections

... a faithful perspective from the past

When people ask me what my favourite prayer is, they are sometimes surprised to hear me recite:

Bless, O God my little cow,

with its endearing second verse:

Bless O God each teat.
bless, O God, each finger,
God bless every drop
which falls into my pitcher.

Delightful, isn't it? And it comes from an era when probably only one in seven people went to church, though over two thirds would have said they were Christians or espoused Christian values.

It was an era when helmsmen rather than chaplains blessed new boats and when midwives as well as priests baptised newborn babies.

The Celtic period in British Church history thrived between the fifth and the seventh centuries and lingered on in outlying areas until well after the Reformation.

It helps to put a perspective on a survey published yesterday which suggested that there was a large disparity between avowal of religious belief and church attendance. One could, of course, say analogously that there is a disparity between the minority of people who attend football matches, and the number of people who avow interest in the sport.

But I'll keep with the old Celts and their prayers about milking, taking eggs from the hen, and putting babies to the breast.

Theirs was a world in which people often believed without the regular benefit of clergy and without an abundance of church buildings. So what they ingested by way of biblical truth and spiritual insight had immediately to be enfleshed in their everyday life.

What happened when the churches grew larger in geographical spread and self-importance was that they developed traditions, strictures, a phalanx of officials and a distinctive culture and vocabulary ... all of which survived as long as the churches had political power and could use moral coercion.

I want to suggest that, in a secular world, the perceived self-obsession of religious establishments with more of a theme-park mentality than a world-affirming mindset alienates people. It's not that they are irreligious. Rather they question loyalty to establishments whose engagement with political economy and global warming seems as limited as their ability to address breast-feeding or hand-milking.

And the issue for people of faith is whether God favours enclosures filled with harmless piety, or whether God – as the Bible often illustrates – has jumped out of the safe space to speak to and through people on the periphery.

15 Nov 05

press freedom

Demonstrating principles
... when guaranteed to antagonise

How do you demonstrate your principles?

Take the principle of democracy, fundamental to and beloved of British society. Supposing someone suggested that to show the rest of the world how democratic we are, there should be a day when at polling stations throughout the country everybody could vote Yes or No to the question: Do you believe in democracy?

Most people would condemn that as a futile and irritating, not to say expensive, exercise which would degrade rather than commend democracy.

How, then, do you demonstrate the principle of freedom of speech? ... by embarking on an equally futile and irritating diversion such as publishing inflammatory cartoons just to prove you can?

What the French satirical magazine *Charlie Ebdo* did yesterday is a far cry from the more naive action of the Danish newspaper which originally printed the offensive cartoons three months ago.

There's no good reason for any press to re-publish material proven to incite violent demonstrations and lead to damage to property, redeployment of troops and closure of embassies. It seems to me to be a wholly gratuitous exercise.

One wonders whether the same publication would be as quick

to print cartoons satirising the suffering of Jews in the Holocaust, the mental agony of people who have been sexually abused or the restricted mobility of Nelson Mandela.

I speak as someone who loves satirical and political cartoons. There's something about that art form which is more eloquent than an editorial in its ability to challenge and change perceptions.

But subversive depiction is not limited to the *Charlie Ebdo*s of the world. It's also a feature of the Christian Gospels – not that Jesus drew cartoons, but he did know the value of cameo stories which could turn received wisdom on its head.

The most famous of these cameos is the parable of the Good Samaritan, in which the maligned and mistrusted foreigner becomes the compassionate benefactor. Another similar and eminently cartoonable story is that of two men praying in the temple. In it, God takes more notice of the faltering phrases of a guilt-ridden tax collector than the practised platitudes of a prince of religion.

What is it that ultimately heals the world – the demonisation of what many people call sacred purely to illustrate the principle of free speech, or the recognition of virtue in people who are routinely derided?

If principles of justice are being weighed, will the scales tip in favour of *Charlie Ebdo* or the Good Samaritan?

9 Feb 06

Corporate judgement

... regarding what makes God angry

Last weekend I was asked an unusual question by a lady at a conference in Preston: 'Why do we not hear much about the wrath of God today?'

Why indeed? Is it that God has gone soft? Or are Christian preachers trying to make God sound more user-friendly than their Muslim counterparts? Or is there something political behind it ... yes political.

You see, the popular perception of God's wrath has to do with divine disapproval of personal behaviour, usually to do with sexuality and usually based on a handful of texts pulled from different parts of the Bible.

But read the book itself and you find that divine wrath is primarily directed at nations and societies regarding the way we communally deal with the marginalised, the economically and socially disadvantaged, the disabled and prisoners.

Yes ... prisoners. Two evenings ago a film was premiered in Berlin. It is based on the personal experiences of three young men from Tipton wrongly imprisoned in Guantanamo Bay. It is, of course, a subjective account, but is perhaps as close a depiction of the truth as is possible, given the US government's reticence to disclose much about their offshore detention centre.

A United Nations report published today underscores this suspect secrecy. The UN envoys interviewed ex-detainees, but were not allowed to visit the five hundred prisoners presently incarcerated. Because they have yet to be put on trial, no one knows how many might be as innocent as the Tipton Three.

But a clear cause for concern are the allegations made of cultural insensitivity, physical and mental abuse and forced feeding ... and this happening on an island deliberately chosen because it is outside the jurisdiction of American courts.

The Bible knows quite a lot about imprisonment. Half of St Paul's correspondence was written from that experience, and the Book of Revelation is a coded letter from an exile on an island to people who were being persecuted by their political masters.

But most poignant is Jesus' parable of the Day of Judgement in which it is not individuals who are pilloried for their moral peccadilloes. Rather, nations are gathered before God's throne, and people are sent to heaven or hell depending, among other things, on how prisoners have been treated.

The justice of God cannot be the pawn or possession of political administrations. Where prisoners are wrongfully detained, God is their advocate and the adversary of their captors.

16 Feb 06

The divine art of improvisation

... being a corrective to human certainty

I met Lucien Zell the other day in a cafe in Prague. He looked bohemian and indeed he was, though not in terms of his ethnic origins. He's a poet and a singer in a rock band.

It was the poet bit that interested me, the more so when I began to read some of his work and conjecture what was behind it.

There were various allusions to God – that fitted well with his being Jewish. Several poems concerned children – which was to be expected, given that he has three of them.

Travelling was another prevalent image. That could be explained by his itinerant lifestyle. And an unabashed sense of vulnerability pervaded his writing which I attributed to his being born with only one hand.

So I developed theories about how his different attributes were responsible for his poetry. And then I thought: but surely there are other disabled, religious itinerants in the world, but they don't all write poetry. So my theorising had to be set aside. It was not the full story.

I was musing over this on the flight back to Scotland, when I read in a newspaper how in British universities the debate about Darwinism versus Creationism is heating up. Here we have alleged scientific theory and deeply held religious belief both purporting to explain the origins of the species.

The most rabid proponents of both Darwinism and Creationism tend to take very polarised positions on the matter, but need this be so?

For it seems to me that here we have two languages with different intentions. One is the language of science concerned with process. It is an ever-changing and intrinsically imprecise language because new discoveries can force established theories to be revisited.

And the other is the language of faith, primarily concerned not with process but with purpose and meaning. It is also an intrinsically imprecise language as St Paul pointed out, for our knowledge of the purposes of God will always be partial this side of time.

Is it beyond the realms of possibility that these two ever-changing perspectives on life might complement rather than threaten each other?

As with my take on Lucien Zell's poetry, theories of origin have a validity of their own. They are analytical, but they are not the whole story. Creativity has a mystery about it. And at the end of the day you can't dissect a mystery, you can only embrace it as I embraced this delightful quatrain of the poet in the Prague cafe:

I used to believe in God's plan,
until I arrived at a great surprise:
God has no plan ...
He prefers to improvise.

23 Feb 06

Becoming what we sing

... inspiration or opiates for the people

When Jacob Zuma, the South African vice-president, was acquitted of rape charges on Monday, he broke into a Zulu song which, roughly translated, means 'Bring me my machine gun'. In so doing, he joined ranks with an illustrious range of people associated with propagandist lyrics.

One of them is Bruce Springsteen who, as reported on the *Today* programme yesterday, has just produced an album which includes songs critical of the current US administration.

A century before Bruce, there was Cecile Frances Alexander, an Anglican bishop's wife who not only penned *All Things Bright and Beautiful,* but in the same poem gave divine approval to the prevailing social order by suggesting that God had preordained:

The rich man in his castle,
the poor man at his gate.

Further back yet there was King David who, though not the author of the Book of Psalms, certainly sang some of their texts which called for the overthrow of current political enemies, particularly the Edomites and Philistines.

Songs are never neutral, whether they are sung in churches, folk clubs or concert halls. They shape what we think about ourselves, God and global issues, and may even influence what we buy. Needless to say, in a previous era some television viewers would have changed their toothpaste of choice on

the strength of a catchy advertising jingle which proclaimed:
You'll wonder where the yellow went
when you brush your teeth with Pepsodent.

The ability of songs to inform and sometimes inflame goes largely unnoticed. Springsteen is quoted because he is so exceptional. But in the sixties and seventies there was a raft of chart-topping artists like Bob Dylan, Joan Baez, Peter, Paul and Mary, and Pete Seeger who inveighed against war, protested for civil rights, and provided songs which shaped public opinion. Even the musical *Hair* was, in part, polemic against the Vietnam war.

If I had one criticism about contemporary songs in both their religious and secular guises, it would be that sophistication in style sometimes disguises the banality of the words.

Given the state of the world, neither religious hymns nor popular songs can afford to inoculate people against reality. If sacred and secular texts do not address war and global warming, over-consumption and endemic poverty, the plight of refugees and the indifference of the privileged classes, neither God nor humanity is served.

Opiates can be aural as well as oral.

10 May 06

Emerging hope in the Emerald Isle

... changed days in Northern Ireland

Twenty-five years ago, the Iona Community helped to bring groups of Catholic and Protestant teenagers from Northern Ireland to Glasgow.

I remember watching with amazement as boys and girls of working age spun round the revolving doors of Boots the Chemist and chased each other in and out of Woolworths with shrieks of infantile delight.

It wasn't until I visited Belfast later that year that I understood why. At that time it was impossible to enter a department store in the middle of Belfast without being searched. It was a fearful period.

I remember coming out of a post office one day and looking right into the barrel of a gun mounted on a security vehicle that was patrolling the city centre. 'The Troubles' was indeed a euphemism.

Northern Ireland is a very different place now and more people from mainland Britain should witness it. Belfast is a lovely city with great architecture, a vibrant night-life, a beautiful waterfront development, a genial café culture. And in my regular visits there, I've yet to hear people of loyalist or republican sympathies desperate to return to the 'good old days' when a job for a boy might depend on the name of his primary school and a job for a man on the nature of his handshake.

So it is to be hoped that the recently recalled Northern Irish

Assembly will attend to the present aspirations of a more relaxed electorate than to the tribal histories of the past.

And perhaps, since people of all sides claim different affiliations to the Christian faith, that best-known of Jesus' parables – the Good Samaritan – might encourage their co-operation.

It was a lawyer who asked him who was the neighbour he was supposed to love. And Jesus told a story, the gist of which is that the neighbour we are called to love is the one whom we have previously vilified but who is capable of doing more good than ourselves.

Whether or not this story which celebrated the kindness of a Samaritan – for whom read Catholic or Protestant or asylum-seeker or whoever is your current *bête noire* – pleased the curious lawyer, we don't know. Possibly not.

For Jesus had the habit of annoying his own people by the way he spoke of those they suspected.

The first assassination attempt on him happened when he told his own home congregation that history indicated how God sometimes favoured not the chosen but those whom the chosen had rejected. His intention was to celebrate the potential in the enemy rather than rehearse the deficiency.

Wouldn't it be great if the DUP and Sinn Fein and all the other parties took the risk of maximising each other's promise rather than exacerbating each other's pain?

17 May 2006

Doing the blessed civil thing

... and the antagonism it breeds

Last weekend I accepted an invitation to an event about which I was personally apprehensive. It was the blessing of a civil partnership.

It involved two people of the same sex and their children. It happened in a church with over a hundred family members and friends surrounding them.

The couple pledged their loyalty to each other and to their children before God, and the children prayed for this new family. I have rarely been at weddings which had the same clear level of faith, moral seriousness, intentionality and community affirmation. And as the ceremony went on I felt within myself blind prejudice being replaced by deep admiration as vulnerable and previously stigmatised people celebrated their love.

The issue of blessing civil partnerships was a lively issue yesterday in Edinburgh, at the Church of Scotland's General Assembly. It used to be that the Church thought it could tell parliament what to do regarding family matters. But parliament, having approved civil partnerships, has created a dilemma for the Church, especially when its ministers are asked by same-sex Christian couples to bless their union.

Inevitably, when discussing such an issue, quotations from scripture are batted about like ping-pong balls, as people of different theological positions try to convince each other of what God or St Paul really meant.

But, as I listen to such debates, I am reminded of other moments in civil and ecclesiastical history where scripture became, if not the whipping boy, then certainly the common crutch for diametrically opposed debaters.

When the place of women in the church and society was discussed in the post-war period, two different understandings of social anthropology were attributed to the Bible. One in which women were co-equal with men, one in which they were subordinate.

Go back two centuries to the anti-slavery movement and you find clerics defending that most inhuman bondage, and others attacking it, all claiming biblical justification.

Whether it be slaves or women or homosexual couples, I suspect that behind the most rabid of opinions is the desire to retain power in the hands of those who are used to it, and to forbid full engagement in the church and society to those who are vulnerable or stigmatised.

One central insight of Christian teaching is that power is never morally neutral. Those who wield it to discriminate against the vulnerable may, in God's sight, be the most morally tarnished.

24 May 06

Charity really begins at home

... otherwise it costs the earth

An illogical thought came to mind yesterday when I heard that unless the growth of cheap air travel is curbed, it could eventually account for 25% of the greenhouse gases created by the United Kingdom. 'The cheapest costs the most,' I suddenly thought ... and then began to test the thesis.

It's certainly true with regard to air travel. The popularity of cheap flights not only ruins the atmosphere, it also negates the effect of more terrestrial green activities.

Any virtue I feel in switching to unleaded petrol or using energy-saving light bulbs is completely obliterated by a cheap flight to London. It's like a weight-watcher buying a diet Cola before tucking into a 2,000-calorie meal.

But the claim that the cheapest costs the most is not just limited to budget travel.

Yesterday several newspapers published an open letter asking the government to call to account companies who promote cheap merchandise sourced in the developing world. As the recent documentary film *China Blue* illustrates, a pair of trendy denim jeans which sell here for £15 to £20 may have come from a sweat-shop in Asia which has been required to accept a tenth of that sum for the product.

We, the purchasers, get the bargain, but the real cost is born by the workers. And if someone should argue 'at least they get a job', the rejoinder must be 'Yes ... but we could afford to pay them more.'

It's a Dives and Lazarus scenario – that's one of Jesus' parables in which the rich man in his castle is aware that there's a poor man at his gate, but does nothing to alleviate the poverty.

No, actually it's worse than that. For we in Britain are not simply aware that global warming and trade injustice are realities ... we actively encourage them by our unchecked appetite for consumption. And it is the wealthiest who have to make the first move.

With regard to air travel, most people who opt for budget airlines come from the higher income brackets. With regard to cheap trendy clothing, it's not the poorest who are the biggest bargain hunters.

I wish sometimes there was a political party which would say: we will curb avarice rather than encourage it; we will limit consumer spending rather than increase it; we will show costly respect for the environment and trade justice rather than publish reports.

That would be to build the New Jerusalem.

That would be to fulfil the dreams of Isaiah and Hosea and Jesus and all people of good faith who know that the real charity which begins at home has to do with the affluent opting to live on less.

17 Oct 06

Fiscal privilege
... or the potential joy of paying taxes

I wonder whether, in the wake of the Sir Nicholas Stern's report on climate change, there might be a new mantra even in the minds of the non-religious:
'Lead us not into global warming,
but deliver us from green taxation.'

Taxation seems to be the popular remedy for many current social disorders. It ranges from traffic congestion charges to a proposed levy on alcohol to discourage teenage drinking.

Now the government, in concert with other political parties, suggests that to halt global warming some form of green tax will need to be introduced ... leading some commentators to accuse the Treasury of avarice.

This tendency to demonise tax (along with the promise of politicians in election years to deliver us from fiscal burdens) has to be challenged. To pay tax is not a penalty, it is a privilege if you can afford it ... and most of us can. More than that, if it enables the hungry to be fed, the sick to be healed, the prisoners to be treated decently, then it is a gospel imperative to which Christians certainly should not object.

But when tax is used as a deterrent – to reduce alcohol abuse or CO_2 emissions, it is inequitable. We don't need expensive research projects to tell us that people bent on drinking excessively will risk poverty to buy liquor whatever the price. And those who have elevated car ownership to the status of a human right will always drive rather than walk to prove their liberty no matter the cost of petrol.

But more than that, the higher up the economic ladder you go, such taxes do not hurt. The executive who delights in corporate hospitality and insists on a Daimler will be much less affected by a green or an alcohol tax than the single mother who drives a mini and has one glass of rosé a day.

Taxation is a partial and potentially unfair response. What we need is legislation which says, 'You can't do this ... even if you can afford it, because the world can't afford to subsidise your level of consumption.' Rationing got Britain through the war and what we are faced with now is something potentially more destructive than all the conflicts of the 20th century put together.

But more than that, we have to foster the simple belief that being kind is a good thing. It's at the heart of all religions ... as when Jesus says,

There must be no limit to your goodness,
since your heavenly Father's goodness knows no bounds.

To care for the earth, to share its resources, to limit our excesses, to pay equitable taxes ... these things are not just necessary, they are good. And this is the era when, as never before, we have to act for goodness' sake.

1 Nov 06

Admission of guilt

... and the difficulties of public penitence

Of all the things I dreaded as a child, the worst was being forced by my mother to appear at the door of a neighbour who I had foulmouthed and say I was sorry. Acknowledging my guilt internally was easy; admitting it to the offended one was a different story.

So, I wonder whether the same childhood trauma is behind the Prime Minister's reticence to apologise for Britain's involvement in the slave trade.

Or is it rather that we cannot translate an individualistic into a corporate ethic. I can apologise to my neighbour, but Lowland Scotland cannot apologise to Highland Scotland for being complicit in the clearances.

On the one hand there is no national or regional consensus, and on the other those in government may be the linear descendants of their predecessors but they do not necessarily extol the same politics or prejudices as those in power centuries ago.

And yet somewhere even in the most secular of psyches is the echo of an injunction: Forgive us our sins as we forgive those who sin against us. It seems to be implicit in these words of Jesus that our full humanity and our faith – if we espouse one – is dependent on our collective ability to own the wrong we have done.

Of course, some will say that if you admit culpability you open the doors to litigation. And when people start suing for the sins of the past, there's no stopping it. Should the southern Irish sue the British for negligence during the potato famine? Should the Gaels sue the English speakers for subjugating their language and culture?

Perhaps the United Nations should frame some resolution which indicates a cut-off point after which financial restitution cannot be claimed.

In the meantime, some light may be shed from the South African experience where the evil of apartheid had to be dealt with ... though not everyone was keen.

In Pretoria last year, I learned that when the Commission chaired by Desmond Tutu was set up, blacks wanted truth and reconciliation but most whites only wanted reconciliation. It seems as if their collective subconscious found admitting the truth to the victims as awkward as I found apologising to my childhood neighbours.

We can't, as a nation, deny gross acts of inhumanity which our forebears perpetrated on powerless people. Nor can we all feel the remorse which *they* should have felt. But we can admit to the truth of the suffering which our nation's imperialist exploits visited on others at home and abroad.

If we don't, we will never be reconciled.

If we don't, we might engage in the same iniquity again, for as Berthold Brecht said of Hitler,
   The bitch that bore him is still in heat.

30 Nov 06

The corrective in Christmas
... and in all religious festivals of good will

Today is Thursday, but I don't hear many people objecting. At least I haven't noticed anyone in Glasgow ripping calendars from office walls in protest against the workplace being invaded by a religion which not everyone espouses.

I mean, Thursday celebrates Thor, the god of weather and crops. And Thor was the son of Odin or Woden, the god of war, education and poetry, whose name is honoured every Wodensday or Wednesday. Such revelations tempt me to exclaim, 'By Jove!' But that would offend countless millions who don't want to be reminded that Jove or Jupiter is the god of oaths, treaties and marriages.

It's not just Christmas trees, flashing stars and civic nativity scenes that are suspect. For the sake of linguistic purity we'll have to go the second mile ... except that would be quoting Jesus and non-believers would demand we say goodbye (or God be with you) to all that!

If you think this is an allusion to the annual displacement activity of taking Christ out of Christmas, you're dead right. But it's not because Christmas needs to preserved as the prime opportunity for the churches to engage in furtive evangelism via Bing Crosby's voice and charity greeting cards.

No, I would want to defend Christmas as I'd defend Hanukkah or Ramadan or any comparable religious festival of a celebratory nature. For it seems to me that they have a humanitarian potential in reminding us of realities such as love, justice and generosity which transcend mundaneness and egocentricity.

And I believe that such festivals which can include and enhance the lives of believers and non-believers alike are increasingly necessary as the economies of the western world offer an alternative and much more sinister pantheon of deities for honouring.

Some of these deities hide behind advertised products I would not be allowed to mention here on air. But if I ask who comes to mind when I speak of:

fulfilment through eating fast foods,

or

success through having brand-named clothing ...

you'll know the kind of allurement I'm referring to. And you might also recognise that encouraging people to believe that having is more important than being is a much more socially exclusive activity than erecting a Christmas tree or hanging up tinsel.

To speak from a purely Christian perspective, a festival like Christmas which is centred on peace, humility and generosity is hardly a threat to a profit-driven secular society which can fund a foreign war but cannot eradicate child poverty.

It is not a threat, but it might be a corrective.

7 Dec 06

money

The third member of the trinity

... following reports of excessive wage hikes and seasonal
bonuses for the financially secure

There's sex
and there's death
and then there's money.

Each holds a fascination for us, each may represent an area of
personal vulnerability, but you can almost guarantee that one
or more of them will be on the front pages of the newspapers
any day.

It's curious how – as distinct from our Victorian ancestors –
sex is up for public discussion and dead bodies, it would seem,
are up for public dissection. Taboos have been turned on their
heads.

But as regards money, we are ambivalent.

We all have some, and we would all like more.

Most of us are resentful when a proportion of our income is
taken from us as tax, and when it comes to the national
budget or the chancellor's assessment of the economy, we are
all opinionated. Hence the barrage of armchair and boardroom criticism in the wake of his recent decision to borrow
rather than tax.

Yet few of us, I venture to suggest, are really open about
money.

We may feel compelled to comment on national fiscal policy, but we would be much more reticent to discuss openly how much we earn, and whether we see money as a moral issue ... as much as sex or death.

Oh we may recognise the morality in increasing or cancelling the debt of developing nations. But is there no moral issue in fiddling company expenses – getting the travel agent to supply a receipt for a full cost fare while flying on a budget airline? Is there no moral issue in grudging a wage rise for public service workers yet applauding the ability of a CEO to secure a bonus that reads like a telephone number at Christmas?

Is there no moral issue in multinational companies avoiding paying a fair wage to workers in Asia and at the same time evading taxation in countries where their sales make most profit?

Indeed is taxation not a moral issue through which the financially privileged ensure among other things that the hungry are fed and sick are cured and the poor are provided for?

If that seems vaguely biblical, it is because the line comes from that most materialist of creeds, the Christian Gospel. If you were to excise what the Bible says about money you'd be left with a book which was more holey than gorgonzola cheese.

What Christianity and Judaism do not teach is that money is filthy lucre. They see it as something which deserves serious moral consideration in terms of truth, justice and decency, as much as death, as much as sex.

Prepared but not broadcast, January 03

Women's troubles

... most of which are caused by men

I was having a conversation about Mary with a group of women from the East End of Glasgow. We were reflecting on how the mother of Jesus is invariably depicted as a sallow-skinned, eternally passive icon of anorexia.

One of the women could hardly contain herself. 'I'll tell you the reason for this,' she said.

'Who is it who paints the pictures of Mary? – men.
Who is it who makes all the statues? – men.
Who is it who writes the songs about Mary? – men.
And they make her out to be such a spineless wee wimp in the hope that their wives will follow Mary's example!'

... that deep spiritual insight came to mind yesterday when I read about how the Equal Opportunities Commission has published yet another report which indicates how women are still massively under-represented in positions of civil and business responsibility.

Some people may regard this as a women's problem or a women's issue, but I have a strong suspicion that we're using the wrong epithet. The women's issue has actually to do with men. It is not that women are less able, less accomplished. It is that men are unwilling to abandon their self-perpetuating male hegemonies. And sometimes I understand why.

When I see drunken businessmen, late in the evening, board-ing trains in Liverpool St Station, heading home to long-suffering wives who have to deal with the habitually sodden beneficiaries of corporate hospitality, I can well imagine that such men would not want to sit across the boardroom from women. They might remind them of the intelligence in their wives which they try hard to avoid.

When I look at males who have been waited on hand and foot by their mothers since birth, while their sisters have had been expected to do all the work about the house, I can well imagine that such men would not instinctively see or want women to be their co-equals.

Admittedly there is, from time to time, female complicity in buttressing the man's world and male self-esteem, even when it is undeserved. But the restoring of the true balance has to be done by men.

I talk about the true balance because I speak from the context of a belief shared by at least three of the major world religions, that when God made humanity, both male and female were created in the divine image.

There wasn't a higher proportion of that image which was masculine, and perhaps men will never discover what it means to be fully human until the God-ordained balance is restored.

How long must 50% of humanity have to wait for those of us who are men to forfeit our bogus superiority? Their and our true humanity depends on it.

Prepared but not broadcast, Jan 04

Where ignorance is not bliss

... in respecting the stranger

Do Americans speak louder than other people, or does it just seem that way?

I was pondering this existential conundrum yesterday morning at 4 am, just off the tip of Greenland.

I was flying from Chicago to London, and in front of me two US citizens were endlessly and volubly discussing risk capital. To my right, one of their compatriots, bedecked with earphones, was watching a film and occasionally erupted with laughter, oblivious to the passengers around him who were trying to sleep.

The observation of a Latin American theologian came to mind:
'To understand a people,
it is not enough simply to know their language.
You also have to comprehend their silence.'

I deeply longed for my garrulous fellow-travellers to do just that.

However, any animosity was tempered by the newspaper article I endeavoured to read. It concerned a curious adventure in the Californian desert.

At the centre of the article was a surprisingly atypical but welcome comment by Brigadier General Robert Cane, a US Army training centre commander.

He said,

> 'The notion that you can fight a war in a foreign country and not know anything about the people or the customs is not acceptable.'

We should warmly commend the US army for its new-found cultural sensitivity, but not limit respect for an alien culture to the theatre of war.

Perhaps if Christian missionaries in the past had been more aware of the importance of the drum to Africans, it would not have been condemned as an instrument of the devil.

Perhaps if Western economists had been more cognisant of the cultures of developing nations, there would, today, be fewer third-world countries coping with unpayable debt.

It is to the credit of Jesus – if one can dare say such a thing – that in his frequent dealings with foreigners, he never presumed to foist his Jewish norms on them. Indeed, when he met a non-Jewish woman at a well, he deliberately disregarded a number of conventions which would have alienated her from him.

For Jesus, respecting the culture was an integral part of respecting the person.

Prepared but not broadcast, Dec 04

Sex is an anti-social activity

... especially among teenagers

It seems that there is a need to teach primary school children about contraception, according to a report from the Institute of Public Policy Research. British teenagers, we are told, have the highest birth rate in Europe because they are the most sexually active. So the solution is not just to tell pre-pubescents about the birds and the bees but also about condoms and the pill.

On a purely pragmatic basis, in order to stop unwanted pregnancies, this may seem a reasonable proposal, but as a policy to improve the lives of teenagers I think it is a retrograde step ... for the simple reason that sex is anti-social.

That might not be the adjective which immediately comes to mind with regard to sexual intimacy. There are plenty of others – pleasurable, fulfilling, deep, orgasmic, mind-blowing. I don't disagree, but I would still want to call sex anti-social, and essentially and profoundly so.

It is something which couples engage in privately. It is neither a spectator sport nor a community activity. It finds its greatest fulfilment when two people who love each other abandon themselves to each other in erotic physical intimacy. It's the kind of thing waxed eloquent about by the book in the Hebrew scriptures called The Song of Songs or The Song of Solomon:

Your navel is a rounded goblet
that will never lack wine;

your breasts are like clusters of grapes. (Ch 7:2&7)

These are not words addressed to a crowd but to a single beloved. Lovemaking is anti-social.

And I want to venture that one reason why the pregnancy rate for Britain's teenagers is highest in Europe is because they are increasingly groomed to live individualistic lives seeking individualistic pleasures rather than enjoying healthy social and communal relations.

I say this with some conviction because last week I spent time with a primary teacher who is responsible for 7- and 8-year olds. I asked her what she found most frustrating about her job, expecting her to talk about changes in government policy. But no. She talked about how difficult it was to get children to stop being sponges soaking up things mindlessly, rather than interacting with the teacher and their peers.

And she identified the root cause of this as homes where video games, computers, gameboys dominate in preference to the integrative activities of family conversation, and playing with kids in the street.

I began to wonder whether this kind of social exclusion masquerading as kindness would be proscribed by Jesus who wanted children to be welcomed in community rather than marginalised.

Maybe it's a naive thought, but I'm becoming more convinced that the encouragement of social intercourse among adolescents might lessen the frequency of the other variety.

Prepared but not broadcast, Oct 06

Politics, passion and the human soul

– a semi-autobiographical reflection

Politics, passion and the human soul

I was recently conducting a retreat mostly for clergy in Leicestershire, and during one session invited people to divide their life into four quarters which would vary in length according to their age. They then reflected on what their dominant understanding or experience of God was in each quarter.

It was a very interesting exercise. Indeed, it was hard to get people to stop, not because they were indulging in anecdotalism, but because many were were identifying their spiritual journey for the first time.

The other day I did this exercise myself, not so much with my understanding of God, but with my understanding of the relationship between faith and politics ... and found distinct differences in the four quarters of my life.

Four quarters of faith and politics

1st quarter: 00–14

Until my mid-teens, politics and religion had little connection. Indeed they seemed antithetical.

My grandfather told stories of the poverty he and his family had known at the end of the 19th century:
- stories about material deprivation which required him to go to school dressed in little more than his sister's nightgown;
- stories of the miserable conditions under which miners like himself worked with no recourse to complaint;
- stories of the savagery of the First World War in which he

lost a brother, whose death my grandfather mourned until the day he died;
- stories of how he as a road mender would cycle up to ten miles through the rain only to find the work had been called off ... and because there was no work, there was no pay;
- stories of how he lost his job and earned a reputation as a troublemaker because he had tried to start a trade union among road-menders.

He was a man of principle, so much so that in the mid '60s when Ian Smith declared UDI in Rhodesia, and Kilmarnock football club, of which he was a life-long supporter, decided to play a Rhodesian team, he vowed he would never watch them again because of their complicity in racism ... and this from a man who had probably never met a black African in his life.

But nothing here about the church or about the practice of religion. My grandfather had never regarded the Christian faith as anything other than anodyne escapism.

2nd Quarter: 15–28

In my second quarter, faith and politics joined hands.

It was partly because I heard and read George MacLeod, the founder of the Iona Community and a passionate pacifist, claiming that possession – never mind use – of nuclear weapons was against the will of the living God.

He declared that which I had not heard preachers saying before, namely that people of faith have to engage in the political processes, that Jesus was not neutral.

MacLeod's passionate assertions fuelled my mind, and were soon underscored by the reading of seminal books:

Malcolm Boyd's *Book of Days*,
Naught for your Comfort by Trevor Huddleston,
Honest to God by John A.T. Robinson,
Bonhoeffer's *Letters and Papers from Prison*.

I began to see faith as something which had to show itself in action. And so I demonstrated against the Vietnam war, and against apartheid and for nuclear disarmament. I brought black students to an all-white youth group, and Roman Catholic friends to speak in unecumenical Protestant churches.

In 1974, I became president of the Students' Council in Glasgow University, and enjoyed staging demonstrations and sit-ins against intransigent university policies, conscientising freshers about the world outside the academic walls. Then just before my term finished, I got arrested and convicted for squatting empty university-owned flats at a time when the growing student population was desperate for accommodation. And all the while, Dietrich Bonhoeffer's *Cost of Discipleship* faced me on my desk.

I believed and believed deeply that to be a committed Christian you had to show faith in action and become involved in the political processes locally and nationally.

3rd Quarter: 29–42

In the third quarter of my life which covers the late '70s to the early '90s I became more complacent as regards matters of social and international justice.

I suppose many of us do, when the comparatively carefree nature of student or early working life is confronted and compromised by the increase in responsibilities ...
– as a spouse or parent for some

- as a carer for elderly or infirm parents for others
- as a manager or head of department
- or just as someone whose working life is so dull or so demanding that a quiet night in front of the television is preferable to canvassing for change.

And I think there also comes a disillusioning suspicion – more noticeable in the USA than in Britain – that idealism and petitioning and demonstrations have little effect on national or international affairs. It's all sewn up and besides, while IBM or Rupert Murdoch might sponsor fringe meetings at political party conferences, what can a Rape Crisis group or an Adult Single Homeless campaign do in comparison to influence the decision-makers.

And I suppose, more objectively, one could look back at the mid-'70s to early '90s and, as regards Britain, not identify much in the life of the churches which pointed up the possible connection between professed faith and political life.

Of course there will be glorious exceptions, such as Archbishop Runcie's denunciation of war at the Falklands service in St Paul's Cathedral. But it seems to me that in the era which confirmed the decline in both public respect for religion and attendance at public worship, the churches turned in on themselves and began to be obsessed with management of resources and aspects of alleged belief which do not enjoy a high profile either in general scriptural witness or in the specific teaching of Jesus.

And we are still involved in that displacement activity of which the current quagmire regarding people of homosexual orientation is a glorious example.

On this issue, there seem to me to be two basic truths we have to contend with. The first is that the Bible does not speak volubly or consonantly on the issue. The alleged plethora of texts disapproving of homosexuality has been narrowed down to six, none of which is directly related to any other, and many of which are increasingly regarded as dealing with prostitution or perversity but not with committed love.

The other basic truth is that God – despite inquisitions and imprecations – still allows gay people to be born as a significant proportion of the population.

Yet in the face of what the Bible says about
  – debt
  – imperialism
  – racism
  – social exclusion
  – ecology
  – and peacemaking

this is the issue which generates most steam and threatens to tear apart a communion and communities.

My only insight as to this imbalance comes from a meeting I once had with a well-known local councillor in Glasgow. She was called Janey Buchan and I met her after she had come from a fractious meeting of the city's education department.

She was irate because at the meeting a request for the refurbishment of a school swimming pool at a cost (in 1975) of around £90,000 had been approved on the nod. The next item on the agenda was a proposal to buy three electric typewriters at £60 each for the department office. For half an hour councillors grunted and groaned at this extravagance.

Janey made the interesting observation that the reason for

this disparity in expended passion was that most people knew something about a typewriter, but nobody could query the cost or process of refurbishing a swimming pool.

Analogously we might say that most heterosexual men might have anything from slight nausea to a nightmare at the thought of same-sex relations. Hence they become vituperative from a subjective personal perspective.

But the juices don't flow quite as adversely when it comes to global warming or the arms trade or Britain's behaviour in Iraq.

The '80s were not a good time on a public level for people of faith to become passionate about anything political. Excepting, of course, the occasional but often limp objections raised to the policies of the incumbent of No 10.

We were all – Labour and Tory voters alike – riding on the waves of affluence and egocentrism. And when you elevate greed and hedonism almost to the status of a human right, then those who have a voice will rarely raise it in objection.

We sometimes rightly accuse the previous Soviet Union and its satellites of setting the agenda for religion by infiltrating and intimidating the churches. But I think that under Thatcher and Reagan there was more subtle management of the intersection of faith and public life. The rise of the religious right in the USA saw a benediction given to financing the contra war in Nicaragua – something in clear contradiction to prophetic injunctions against imperialism.

At the same time there was the elevation of the importance of Christian family values ... an exercise in spiritual mythology if ever there was one.

The Methodist grande dame Margaret Thatcher did not have a right-wing ecclesiastical phalanx to bless her policies as Reagan did in the USA. She was keener to promote her own brand of scriptural exegesis, as when she told the General Assembly of the Church of Scotland that the Good Samaritan could not have been so generous had he not profited from a free enterprise culture.

There was an episode during her reign when radical religion made the BBC news. In Glasgow some of my colleagues organised a church service in protest against the Poll-Tax, that great egalitarian measure whereby the single rich man in his castle paid the same rate of local authority taxation as the poor man, his wife and every one of his unemployed adult progeny in the damp basement flat near the castle gate.

It was a great act of worship, with lively singing, people testifying to how the poorest would be hit by this new physical measure, heartfelt prayer and a great buzz about the church. Because it was organised by lay people, there was no cleric who was answerable for the event. For this or whatever other reason, the then Secretary of State for Scotland was wheeled into a radio studio to denounce this 'communist' activity.

But it was not just the churches who became anaemic in the '80s as regards social and international justice. Popular culture had also gone soft where it should have been hard-edged.

I discovered this retrospectively when I had a night free in Minneapolis in 2002. I was there with three younger colleagues, all of whom had been attending a church musicians' conference at which I was speaking.

I noticed in the local press that there was a revival of a '60s' hit musical in town. Its name was *Hair*. I had seen this 'scandalous, sensational' stage production, which included around thirty seconds of nudity, some thirty years previously in Glasgow.

At any rate, we sat through this period-piece performance. All the songs were sung as before, the stage set was distinctly hippieland. But what I had not realised from my first viewing of the show was that it was actually a political musical. It was anti-Vietnam. The hero, if one may call him that, is a boy who is called up for military service. Unlike others, he doesn't burn his draft card or escape to Canada. He goes to Vietnam and gets killed.

At the end of the performance, the house-lights came on as the cast took their final bow. Then one of the actors came to the apron of the stage and said in a very natural voice:

'We discovered earlier today that this city is the place from which came the first female soldier to be killed in Iraq.

'We have also discovered that there's a fund set up in her memory which distributes money to Iraqi children orphaned by allied bombing.

'So the cast decided that each evening we are here during the three-week run, we'll stand in the foyer at the end of each performance with collecting cans should you wish to make a donation to a local charity which will send the money direct to Iraq.'

He stopped and there was a profound hush in the audience, broken only by the sound of weeping, as if men and women by the simple action of these young actors were both being reminded of a radicalism in themselves which had long lain dormant ... and also sensing that for the first time they could make a public sign of their disapproval of the war.

Go back to the '60s and '70s, not because they were good old and glorious days ... go back to the '60s and recognise how in popular music, on the stage and on television, the voices of popular protest and dissent were rehearsing without fear ... Dylan, Baez, Peter, Paul and Mary.

In this present excursion into the Middle East – depending on whether you take 'official figures' or those offered by medics on the ground – we have killed up to one in forty of a nation's civilians in three years of peace ... almost ten times as many as were killed in the 9-year war between Iraq and Iran.

But I have digressed.

4th Quarter: 43+

Let me revert to my four-quarter reflection and note that in the last quarter of my life, the relationship between Christian faith and worldly politics has become, for me, more acute.

Now this could be an age thing. As one gets older, some of the reservations of the middle years are less meaningful. I asked one of the most radical women I know, Dorothy McCrae McMahon, the Australian cleric and activist, if she was enjoying retirement from work.

'Yes,' she replied, 'it's great. I can say exactly what I feel and I don't give a damn for the consequences.'

I'm not quite at her stage yet, but I sense both a new stirring and a different urgency in my bones.

The new stirring is because I have stopped reading the Bible and theology from the top down, but rather from the bottom up.

Belief from the bottom up

Now, what do I mean by this?

I mean that for too long the comprehension of the Christian faith has been captive in the West to arid intellectualism and pussy-footing clericalism. We – whether conservative intellectual or woolliest of liberals – have accorded to disengaged theologians and ecclesiastically constipated priests and ministers a right which they do not deserve, namely to be the primary arbiters of Gospel truth.

The result on the evangelical wing is that salvation by right doctrine has been a substitute for salvation through a lively relationship with Christ. I do not see anywhere in the scripture where Jesus asks people questions on the shorter catechism or scripture knowledge, or where he poses a theological conundrum as a prerequisite for discipleship.

Rather he says,
> *I thank you Father for hiding these things from the learned and wise, and revealing them to the simple.*

On the more liberal wing a similar heresy is bred as some fine theological minds in the States, some of which are totally disillusioned by their experience of religion, offer a kind of humanistic, possibly God-free, assortment of pseudo-beliefs that might get us through the next year or two.

I was recently part of a local church study group where lay people were being exposed to the 'radical' thinking of certain Christian intellectuals regarding Christmas.

One woman put everything in a new perspective when she said,

'I don't know what that bishop is going on about. I mean we all know that there was no snow at Christmas and that the wise men didn't arrive the same night as the shepherds ... but what do we tell the children?'

Opening the Bible through the life of the laity

And then I remembered a page in the Solentiname Gospels from Nicaragua which records the conversation of peasants gathered round a priest who has just read them the story of the Magi. He encourages people to bring their story, their lives, their questions and observations to help open up the text. And after a while, an old peasant farmer says,

'I have just been thinking ... When God called the Wise Men, he sent a star. But when he called the poor shepherds, he sent a choir of angels.

The poor must be God's favourite people.'

I would rather have that reading of the story which energises faith than the intellectual meanderings of the academics more interested in propounding their theories than in advancing God's purposes of redemption.

Let me take another example ... a day in which I was looking at the Psalms with women from Catholic parishes in the north of Glasgow.

We spent the morning on Psalm 23 and discovered ten good reasons why this was the most popular psalm. They had to do with language, imagery, consolation, pictures of God, etc.

In the afternoon, I handed out Psalm 88 which – if you don't know it – is the most despairing poem in the Bible. It begins with a plea for help. It moves through a sarcastic section

115

where the writer asks awkward and impolite questions of God. It ends with the horrendous line,

You have taken friends and family far from me.
Darkness is now my only companion.

We looked at the ten reasons why Psalm 23 was so popular, and not one could be transferred to Psalm 88. So, I asked what people thought of it. And one wee woman who had gone through a major upset in her life said:

'I think it's marvellous.

You see, while I was going through my bad spell there were nearly two years when I would go to church but I'd never take mass. I'd just sit at the back and cry.

If I had known that psalm was in the Bible, I'd have read it every day. Because you wouldn't ask these questions if you didn't believe somebody was listening.'

Here was a reading of the text which did not depend on intricate exegesis, but relied on people at the bottom being enabled to feel that this word of God is for them and can be brought into dialogue with their existence.

This does not undermine the intellectual pursuit of the academically gifted or the theological musings of the parish priest. But what we have to ask is whether such things enable liberation from below or encourage a dependency on enlightenment from above. Theology and preaching are the servants not just of the church but of the world. They are tools to aid God's purposes not icons held up for reverence.

Let me take one other very immediate example.

Last Sunday evening I was engaged in biblical conversation with around 25 people, who included five ministers and two lecturers. The rest were lay people from across the socio-political spectrum.

We were looking at the story of the Tower of Babel. In advance of the conversation, two of the ministers had looked up commentaries so that they would have something to say in confirmation or opposition to my exposition.

But I didn't expound anything. I just took people into the text and then asked them to discover its significance for life today.

I chose this text because it is one of the passages of scripture on the basis of which Afrikaaner theologians underwrote apartheid as a divine mandate. For them God gave people different tongues and different lands as a punishment and they were bound ever to keep apart.

But the people on Sunday night, some of whom live in areas with a range of asylum-seekers, discovered something very different in the text.

Some saw it as indicating that God condemns monuments to human avarice, whether chiselled in stone or formulated in words.

Some saw it as indicating that God did not want a monolithic and monoglottal society. Rather, God intended humanity to be diverse.

One person saw the scattering of people from a place of homogeneous introspection as a blessing.

Another person echoing, unknown to him, the words of the

117

Japanese theologian Kosuke Koyama – said that we needed other languages, other cultures, to understand God. Otherwise God was little more than a projection of the corporate or national ego. (Koyama's words were: The mother tongue is too small.)

The fact of the incarnation should encourage us to expect ... as Jesus expected and illustrated ... that the kind of spiritual discernment that engages faith with existential realities does not emerge from a theory but from connectedness with the people of the earth, particularly those at the bottom.

His outrage ... is there a better word? ... at the scribes and the Pharisees:
Woe to you!
Woe to you!
does not come about because they have just expounded a treatise on the topography of heaven, but because they have failed
   ... *failed* the impoverished,
       the indebted,
       the doubting.

The first attempt on Jesus' life ... which occurs the first time he preaches in his home synagogue ... is not because he has upset people by claiming that the book of Isaiah may have been written by more than one author ... but because he illustrates from two examples in Jewish history that God is known to favour non-Jews, particularly those who are marginalised by poverty or disease.

The crucifixion is not solely the result of Christ claiming for himself equality with God ... the crucifixion happens because
– Christ has spoken of the love of God in the language of the marketplace

- Christ has found in aged widows, foreign soldiers and
  untutored children models of discipleship
- Christ has claimed that in him all that is written in the
  prophets is not abandoned but fulfilled, which means now
  as then that
      land distribution,
      foreigners' rights,
      the equal status of women,
      the arms race,
  ... are not optional extras for a panel discussion followed by
  refreshments, but part and parcel of faithful commitment.

Or am I getting it all wrong?

And did Jesus actually spend endless hours discussing the
eschatological issue and the doctrine of the real presence with
rabbinic disciples who wore fishermen's clothes for Hallowe'en?

The trickle-down effect does not work ...
    neither in economics
    nor in Christian belief.

It must be the bubble-up effect, where the reality or otherwise
of the Gospel is discovered on the ground, not in the sky. Is
that not why, after the ascension, an angel asks the disciples
why they are staring at the sky and not going back to the city?

In exactly the same way as, centuries earlier, Elijah on the
mountain-top did not find in the dizzy heights a soothing
balm, but rather a pregnant silence through which he was
told to get off his backside and re-enter the world from which
he was retreating.

Grounded theology

Lest it be thought that what I am doing here is propounding some kind of anti-intellectualism, this is not the case. The Christian faith is not flabby, the word of God is not saccharine. It can stand up to scrutiny and debate, and it must. But that debate has to be rooted in earthly reality rather than ethereal speculation.

Hence one of my favourite writers is the Jesuit theologian Jon Sobrino, a Salvadorean whose book *Where is God?* is a regular companion. I can hardly get past the foreword ... not because it is obscure, but because it all flows from the mind of one who lives in solidarity with people who have gone through civil war, known the adverse effect of North American meddling in Central American politics, and lived through a natural disaster – namely the hurricane of 2001 – only to see their suffering eclipsed by the more predictable tragedy of 9/11.

Here is a brief extract from the section on Empire ... words which could never be written by anyone on the side of the presumptive masters or victors:

> *Until recently the word* empire *seemed out of date, but the reality has returned. The prostration of the planet as a whole can no longer be described in simple terms of injustice and capitalism. Iraq has made clear there is an empire, and today's empire is the United States.*
>
> *The empire imposes its will directly on the people it is attacking, and indirectly on its coalition allies. But what is more serious in the long run – for it goes far beyond Iraq and today's wars – the empire may succeed in imposing on all humanity its own versions of their reality, their dignity, their happiness. Most fundamentally it*

imposes the primacy of the individual and of success as superior ways of being human, and the selfish and irresponsible enjoyment of life *as an indisputable value. All this without consideration of resources, so that an athlete, singer or movie actor in the United States can be paid the equivalent of a high percentage of the national budget of a country in Sub-Saharan Africa. We mention this disproportion because it is seldom noticed.*

But the victims in those places help us not to be confused about God. He is not the God of the empire. The most courageous believers will tell us: he is the God of the victims. He is the God of Jesus, who was also a victim of the empire.

(Jon Sobrino: *Where is God?* Orbis Books)*

I said earlier that there were two reasons which in my present quarter of life had made the relationship between faith and politics more urgent.

The first was learning from below rather than always from above.

The heresy of dualism

The second was realising that dualism, which is alive and well in some of our churches, is nothing less than a heresy.

What do I mean by dualism? I mean the dividing of life into what is ostensibly sacred and what is suspiciously secular.

---

* English translation © 2004 by Orbis Books, Maryknoll, NY 105450, USA.

Ever since Augustine, and particularly after Calvin, there has been a gradual assent to the belief that there are some things which are properly the business of Christian faith and some which are not.

Among the business items are:
sin,
personal morality,
old people,
children,
hospitals,
starting missions.

Among the items not for business are:
challenging the government,
money laundering,
tax evasion,
the abuse of women,
global warming,
and the reception of missions.

It is partly the result of the building of churches ... structures which I love, yet which have an odd way of indicating that some things belong to God and others don't. This is aided by liturgical language as much as by ecclesiastical architecture.

For example, when – with the exception of 'special services' – did we ever sing a song about the stock market, though its behaviour can make a few instantly rich and many instantly penniless?

When did we last pray about the suited gentlemen in Liverpool St Station who dine out daily in corporate hospitality and enjoy golden handshakes every Christmas, but whose deliberations *vis à vis* the futures market destine countries like Kenya to have minute incremental rises in the price paid for coffee with never a free lunch in sight for anyone beneath the equator.

When did we ever find a liturgy to let us lament over the botch-up of Iraq?

It is a creeping dualism which encourages the belief that some things pertain to Christian belief and others don't. My question is: if God is the Lord of all the nice stuff, which deity is in charge of the nasty?

Undoubtedly religious vocabulary exacerbates the situation ... I mean when did anyone ever sing:
    'Praise to Jesus in the kitchen'?
... although he enjoyed being in kitchens ... of Martha and Mary and many more.
Or
    'Abide with me, here comes a prostitute;
    Keep her far off, and keep me, Lord, astute.'
... though Jesus enjoyed the company of prostitutes much more than that of priests.

The ancient Celts like the ancient Jews could not conceive of a portion of life which was open to God and another portion which was closed. The Jews had prayers for going to the loo, the Celts for putting the baby to breast, milking the cattle, setting out on journeys.

All of life ... domestic, industrial, recreational ... was lived under the aegis of one God for whom nothing was 'dirty' ... and certainly not sex or money. And this is not because of naivety, but because of deep biblical faith ... which again is more evident in the marginalised than in the over-socialised.

Two years ago, when I met Allan Boesak, one of the great South African orators who denounced and exposed the iniquity of apartheid, I asked him why the transition from white to black power had been so incredibly peaceful, with virtually no bloodletting against the previous white administration and its lackeys.

Boesak was quite clear in his own mind. He said,
> 'I believe that ... black and coloured South Africans who believed the Gospel felt convinced that this was the moment when the truth of Christ had to be manifest, that forgiveness had to triumph over hatred, reconciliation over vengeance.'

I have not heard anyone of equal stature within the Western religious and political establishments be so affirmative of the Gospel imperative to love the enemy.

An environmental coda

We do not need to find a new Bible or a new guru; we need to open our eyes to what is already there and act on it. And nothing more so than as regards the number one current threat to humanity, which is commonly agreed to be the despoliation of the earth's environment.

No ... the Bible does not specifically mention the ozone layer or CO_2 emissions. It admits of something much more radical.

It claims that the earth is primarily a trust in our keeping, not a possession for our despoiling.

It claims – as in Jeremiah – that the refusal of nature to

deliver its traditional gifts is a judgement of God on those who use its resources cavalierly, and who plunder its resources to support the obese and indulgent at the expense of nourishing the needy.

And, more than that, it claims repeatedly that the earth is one of three forums or four which offer praise to the Almighty. One is the angel choir in heaven, one is the church on earth, and one is the natural order which engages in a song or symphony of praise primarily for God's delight.

This is not fanciful talk. The Psalms and the prophecy of Isaiah are shot through with it ... and humanity is charged with enabling this litany or liturgy to be as cherished and safeguarded as the best Anglican cathedral choir is at evensong.

It is not simply a matter of 'all things bright and beautiful'. This is stewardship not romanticism, and Christian people should not be bringing up the rearguard in a reluctant bandwagon, but in the forefront of preserving this earth and its people, because God is not going to give us any other.

I alluded a while ago to the centrality of the incarnation in all of this. With no disrespect to people of other faiths, one of the truths which Christianity boldly proclaims is that the Word did not remain a concept or become a theory, but became flesh ... whereby not only each human life but the very fabric of creation is caught up with and in God.

And more than this, the reason behind the incarnation is not something veiled in secrecy. It is encapsulated in that verse of John's Gospel which is most frequently disported in tracts and handbills:

God so loved the world
that he gave his only begotten son

that whosoever believes in him should not perish
but have everlasting life.

Usually associated with the death of Jesus and often used to induce contrition, the astounding revelation with which this fondest of verses begins is often missed by us:

God did not so love human souls
    or the General Synod
    or Vatican II
    or Celtic spirituality
    or the Alpha course.

God so loved the world.

God so loved the world.

Now, is that not something to get passionate about?

(Transcribed from notes for a lecture delivered in Bristol
on 30th November 2006)

The Wild Goose Resource Group

The Wild Goose Resource Group is an expression of the Iona Community's commitment to the renewal of public worship. Based in Glasgow, the WGRG has two resource workers, John Bell and Graham Maule, and a project worker, Jamie Schmeling, who lead workshops, seminars and events throughout Britain and abroad. They are supported by Gail Ullrich (administrator) and Victoria Rudebark (sales & copyright administrator).

From 1984 to 2001, the WGRG workers were also part of the Wild Goose Worship Group. The WGWG consisted of around sixteen, predominantly lay, people at any one time, who came from a variety of occupational and denominational backgrounds. Over the 17 years of its existence, it was the WGWG who tested, as well as promoted, the material in this book.

The task of both groups has been to develop and identify new methods and materials to enable the revitalisation of congregational song, prayer and liturgy. The songs and liturgical material have now been translated and used in many countries across the world as well as being frequently broadcast on radio and television.

The WGRG, along with a committed group of fellow-Glaswegians, run HOLY CITY, a monthly ecumenical workshop and worship event for adults in the centre of Glasgow. The WGRG also publishes a mail-order catalogue, an annual Liturgy Booklet series and a twice-yearly newsletter, GOOSEgander, to enable friends and supporters to keep abreast of WGRG developments. If you would like to find out more about subscribing to these, or about ways to support the WGRG financially, please contact:

The Wild Goose Resource Group, Iona Community, Fourth Floor,
Savoy House, 140 Sauchiehall Street, Glasgow G2 3DH, Scotland.
Tel: 0141 332 6343   Fax: 0141 332 1090
e-mail: wgrg@gla.iona.org.uk   web: www.iona.org.uk/wgrg
www.wgrg.co.uk   www.holycity-glasgow.co.uk